I0521206

THE HUMILITY
YOU WANT
AND THE
WORLD
NEEDS

7 Transformative Tools
for Personal Growth
to Develop Inspiring
Leadership, Improve
Relationships, and
Attain Inner Peace

SCHALEE SANCHEZ

Paperback ISBN: 979-8-9992137-0-9

Hardback ISBN: 979-8-9992137-1-6

Editor: Chisom Ezeh

Cover Design: Schalee Sanchez

Dedication

To Alicia, Iliana, Emilie, and Nathan…

You mean more to me than words could ever express, so my goal every day is to show you.

Table of Contents

Acknowledgments

To Chisom Ezeh, thank you for being an incredible editor. Your insight and skill brought clarity, depth, and meaning to this book, enhancing the experience for every reader.

To Carli Jeffery, Stefan Hettich, and Brittany Oei, I am grateful for your encouragement, input, feedback, and guidance. Your voices were a valuable part of the entire process.

To James Ingrahm, thank you for believing in me and saying yes. You helped make a long-held dream a reality.

To Heather Davila and Keneé Dover, thank you for making it possible for me to discover what my life could be.

To Jessica Hooten, thank you for helping me be bold and relax. Your presence gives me the freedom to show up fully as myself.

To the CG community, thank you for inspiring me to do hard things. Your example and camaraderie constantly push me to excel.

To the K-fit crew, thank you for lightening the load with your laughter and providing steadiness amid unexpected changes. Your friendship means more than you know.

To the reader, thank you for trusting me. I hope these pages offer light, clarity, and a better way forward.

And most deeply, I thank Jesus. You are my unshakable rock through every up and down.

Why I Chose the Dwennimmen Symbol

If you've noticed the symbol on the cover, it's called Dwennimmen, an Adinkra symbol from the Akan people of Ghana. It means *"ram's horns,"* and it represents the balance of strength and humility. I chose this symbol because it captures the heart of everything this book stands for.

The ram is powerful, capable of standing its ground. But even in its strength, it bows its head, not in defeat, but in respect. That's the kind of humility I believe in. Not shrinking. Not silencing yourself. But showing up with unshakable strength, grounded confidence, and a willingness to listen, learn, and serve.

To me, Dwennimmen is a beautiful reminder that humility and power aren't opposites; they belong together. As you walk through these pages and beyond, I hope this symbol reminds you of the strength that lives in gentle leadership and the power of choosing humility again and again.

Introduction

As a child, one of my favorite activities was visiting the library and returning home with a fresh stack of books to explore. I was especially drawn to stories about President Abraham Lincoln, so I eagerly immersed myself in every book I could find about him. His leadership style fascinated me. I wanted to learn everything I could from him. I wanted to grow up to be like him.

At the time, my elementary school mind couldn't quite grasp what made him so extraordinary. But now, looking back with the perspective of decades, I understand it was his profound humility that captured my attention. Lincoln's remarkable ability to listen to opposing viewpoints and thoughtfully weave diverse perspectives into his decisions revealed humility not as a weakness, but as an incredible strength. His leadership not only guided the nation through an extremely turbulent chapter, but also sowed the seeds for healing and reconciliation in its aftermath.

Humility has remained a guiding principle throughout my life, consistently shaping how I define success, approach relationships, lead others, and even understand my own self-worth. Time and again, I've witnessed the profound power of humility and the remarkable impact it can have on the world around us. It's these discoveries that fuel my passion for sharing this journey with you, because I believe that embracing humility has the power to not only transform your life, but to create ripples of change that extend far beyond you, touching families, communities, nations, and future generations.

**Humility isn't about thinking less of yourself.
It's about thinking of yourself less.**

It's not about shying away from your strengths, but about using them for the good of yourself and others. Humility is about balance, awareness, and an openness to learn and grow. It allows us to connect deeply with those around us, fostering genuine relationships and inspiring leadership.

The purpose of this book is to offer you practical tools and insights to cultivate humility across all areas of your life. Whether you're seeking to improve your leadership skills, build stronger relationships, or find inner peace, this book is here to guide you on that path.

We'll explore seven transformative tools that can help you develop humility. Each one offers a unique way to practice and integrate humility into your daily life. While these tools can support other areas of personal growth, our focus will remain on humility.

Before we dive into the tools, I want to share with you an important truth. If you're anything like me, with a Type A personality that craves structure and clear steps from Point A to Point B, you might naturally expect personal growth to follow a straight, predictable path. But one of the most transformative lessons I've learned is this: Growth rarely unfolds in a linear way.

Rather than a direct arrow aimed at a bullseye, growth is much more like a dance, full of side-steps, unexpected turns, and graceful twists. While an arrow follows a single trajectory to reach its target, a dance embraces variety. It can be smooth or dramatic, slow or spirited, sharp or flowing, spontaneous or intentionally paced. This journey of growth will be much more like a dance than a straight shot.

The tools I'll be sharing are yours to use throughout the process, not in a rigid order but as companions along the way. You'll have the freedom to choose when and how to use them. While I'll offer specific prompts for certain areas of growth, there will always be multiple tools available and you'll be empowered to decide which steps feel right for you at each moment.

As you journey through this book, I invite you to engage deeply with its content. Use it as a tool for reflection and action. Try the exercises, answer the questions, and let the stories inspire you to think differently about humility.

Let's begin!

Humility is the gateway into the grace
and the favor of God.

Harold Warner

Chapter 1:

Understanding Humility

Humility is not an easy concept to grasp in today's world, where we're bombarded with messages that tell us to put ourselves first, to shout our accomplishments from the rooftops. But what if true strength lies not in how loudly we proclaim our victories but in how we lift others?

My experiences have taught me that humility is not about diminishing oneself, but rather about recognizing the value in others and the importance of our collaboration. It's about recognizing that we are part of something greater.

Humility in the Modern World: Why It Matters

In our fast-paced society, humility is often overshadowed by aggressive ambition. Those who relentlessly climb to the top often disregard and demean the dignity of others along the way. This culture of arrogance leaves many feeling disconnected, unseen, and undervalued.

The damage this pride and self-promotion have caused is all too obvious. We see people mistreated and oppressed by those who are hungry for power and dominance. Rather than sit back and criticize those who live and lead that way, we are given a choice to infuse the world with the one thing that will triumph over pride: humility.

In the noise of self-promotion, humility is not only relevant—it is vital.

Contrasting sharply with arrogance, humility motivates us to genuinely care for and uplift others. When we approach life with humility, we look for opportunities to serve. We notice how we can contribute to the well-being of others in very specific and significant ways. And most importantly, we are empowered to take action.

Humility frees us from the cage created by constantly focusing on how our actions will affect us, so that we become more concerned about how our actions can benefit those around us. We begin to see and live beyond ourselves.

Humility completely changes our perspectives, just like putting on a new pair of glasses when our vision is 20/80. It opens our eyes to see that our viewpoint is just one among many. This openness enhances our relationships, as we become better listeners and more compassionate companions.

Humility also plays a crucial role in conflict resolution. In situations of tension and disagreement, humility enables us to step back and consider solutions that prioritize mutual respect and understanding. International diplomacy offers numerous case studies where humble leaders achieved breakthroughs by valuing dialogue over domination. By approaching conflicts with humility, they created fertile ground for peace and cooperation.

Humility is a catalyst for innovation and learning. When we accept our limitations and embrace the possibility of failure, we open ourselves to new ideas and perspectives. Life's challenges become opportunities for learning rather than insurmountable obstacles. Humility teaches us to be patient with ourselves and others, fostering an inner peace that transcends external circumstances.

The benefits of humility extend beyond personal growth into professional settings. Humility in the workplace nurtures creativity and drives progress by fostering an environment where experimentation is encouraged and valued.

In leadership, humility is transformative. It invites collaboration and innovation, allowing teams to thrive in an environment where every voice matters. Successful business leaders often attribute their achievements not to their intelligence or charisma but to their willingness to learn from mistakes and seek input from others.

In today's interconnected world, humility is more relevant than ever. It is not merely a personal virtue but a societal necessity. As we grapple with global issues that require collective action and understanding, humility reminds us that progress is achieved not through individual wins but through shared commitment and cooperation.

As you explore the chapters ahead, I invite you to reflect on how humility can positively shape your life. Consider how it might enhance your relationships, strengthen your leadership abilities, or bring you more inner peace. Humility is not a destination but a way of being that enriches every aspect of life. Embrace it with an open heart and mind, ready to discover its profound impact on your world.

Before we go any further, let's look at the tools that we will use throughout this book:

- **Prayer/Meditation**: Finding moments of intentionally communicating with and listening to God.

- **Journaling**: Reflecting on your thoughts and experiences to gain clarity and understanding.

- **Habit Tracking**: Monitoring your behaviors and making intentional changes.

- **Community**: Engaging in relationships with therapists, counselors, coaches, mentors, or safe, trusted friends for feedback, insight, and guidance.

- **Gratitude**: Expressing appreciation and acknowledging the value of others.

- **Affirmations**: Speaking truths and reinforcing positive beliefs about yourself and others.

- **Rest**: Allowing time for stillness and solitude.

Let's unpack them further:

1. **Prayer/Meditation** – Creating time for prayer/meditation is essential for identifying personal biases and areas for growth. They reveal the condition of your heart and enable you to notice whether your responses stem from humility or ego. Pay attention to moments when defensiveness arises—these instances often signal a need for deeper introspection. Recognizing personal biases requires courage, as it challenges our self-perception and invites change. Approach this process with compassion, acknowledging that growth is an ongoing journey. Meditation focused on humility can also be incredibly powerful, centering your thoughts and fostering a mindset of peace and acceptance. Visualize yourself embodying humility in daily interactions, reinforcing this intention through mindful breathing exercises.

2. **Journaling** – In the hustle of everyday life, finding time for journaling might seem like a luxury. Yet, carving just a few moments each day for introspection can cultivate humility in profound ways. Think of daily journaling as a conversation with yourself, where honesty reigns. This practice not only grounds you in humility but also highlights areas for personal growth.

3. **Habit Tracking** – Creating a habit tracking chart is simple. You can use your journal, a separate notebook, or a printed sheet. On each line, write out the action you want to intentionally practice. Beside it, make a column for each day of the week, large enough for a check mark or

the date. Finally, add a column to record observations of what you learn along the way. Repeat the weekly chart until the habit is formed. As you weave this routine into your life, you'll find that humility becomes not just an aspiration but an integral part of who you are. Here's a sample:

Habit	Day 1	Day 2	Day 3	Day 4	Day 5	Day 6	Day 7	Observations
Pause before responding	✓	✓		✓	✓	✓		Felt more peace and patience
Practice active listening	✓		✓	✓	✓		✓	Learned more about my spouse
Apologize for hurting someone		✓					✓	Built deeper trust with my colleague

Note: In Atomic Habits, James Clear emphasizes that habit formation is not about a fixed number of days, but about consistency. While many people refer to the myth of "21 days," Clear highlights a 2009 study from University College London which found that, on average, it takes 66 days for a new habit to become automatic—though the range can vary widely from 18 to 254 days, depending on the complexity of the habit and individual factors. Focus on showing up consistently. Small, repeated actions compound into significant, lasting change.

4. **Community** – Feedback from others offers invaluable insights that self-reflection alone might miss. Constructive criticism sessions can be eye-opening, providing perspectives that challenge your assumptions. Peer feedback workshops are another great way to gather diverse opinions in a supportive environment. Encourage colleagues or friends to share their observations—sometimes an outside view sees what we overlook. Embrace these opportunities with an open heart, viewing feedback not as criticism but as guidance for growth.

5. **Gratitude** – Developing a daily routine of gratitude is essential. Consider establishing an evening ritual where you unwind by remembering specific things you are thankful for. Meditation focused on humility

can also be incredibly powerful, centering your thoughts and fostering a mindset of peace and acceptance. Take a moment to reflect on your day, noting instances where humility shone through.

6. **Affirmations** – Speaking truths and statements of belief each morning further reinforces a humble mindset. Begin your day by saying these statements out loud, like "I value humility." "I will approach today with humility." "I am humble." "I will uplift others." These small steps set a tone of awareness, openness, and direction that lasts throughout your day.

7. **Rest** – Humility makes us keenly aware of our limitations. Moments of stillness and solitude bring us into a state of receiving what we lack on our own. They play a vital role in our transformation and personal growth. They can be experienced in a variety of ways, ranging from small pockets of time throughout the day to extended periods of several days during a retreat.

Embracing humility can transform your life. It improves your relationships by fostering empathy and understanding. It enhances your leadership by creating environments of trust and collaboration. And it brings inner peace by aligning your actions with your values. Imagine the freedom of letting go of the need to always be right and instead, being open to growth and connection.

Transformation Prompt – 2 (Journaling) and 5 (Gratitude)

- Take a moment to think about how humility has influenced your life so far. Consider moments when you felt humbled by an experience or inspired by someone else's humility. Reflect on how these instances have shaped your outlook on life and your interactions with others.

- Think about people in your life who have exemplified humility and express gratitude to them through any preferred method.

Humility:
Dispelling the Myths and Misconceptions

Humility is often perceived as a sign of vulnerability or a lack of assertiveness. It's understandable why this misconception persists, especially in a world that rewards assertiveness and dominance. However, true humility is not about being a pushover or allowing others to diminish your worth. It is about confidently knowing your strengths while choosing to acknowledge and elevate the contributions of others.

Far from weakness, humility is a profound strength that empowers individuals to step back, listen, and learn. It enables us to stand firm in our beliefs while remaining open to new ideas and perspectives. The calm confidence that stems from humility often has a far more enduring impact than flashy charisma or arrogance.

Consider the example of Nelson Mandela, who served as President of South Africa from 1994 to 1999. Mandela's strength lay not in commanding obedience but in his capacity to listen and understand. His leadership, deeply rooted in humility, enabled him to bridge divides and promote reconciliation in a country torn apart by apartheid. Mandela's humility never diminished his authority; it fortified it. He demonstrated that humility is a powerful force in leadership, allowing leaders to connect more deeply with their followers and inspire genuine loyalty and respect.

In today's culture, humility is often eclipsed by an obsession with personal victories and public recognition. Yet those who practice humility often discover that it yields long-term rewards far greater than the fleeting satisfaction of self-promotion. Humility fosters authentic self-reflection, helping us recognize our limitations and opportunities for growth. This self-awareness becomes a wellspring of strength, fueling continuous learning and personal development.

**Humility challenges us to redefine success
in terms of collective achievement rather than
individual accolades.**

I spent much of my life extremely shy and reserved. Yet, humility was my powerful teacher, helping me shift my focus away from my own insecurities and toward the value I can offer to others. It gave me an unexpected boldness to speak up and make decisions in difficult circumstances for the greater good. As I've learned to look beyond outcomes that directly concern me, my strengths and abilities have flourished, equipping me to serve across diverse settings, connect with people from all walks of life, and thrive in different cultures.

One of the beautiful truths about humility is its universality. It knows no boundaries of age, gender, or culture. Anyone, anywhere, can become a conduit of humility and an agent of transformation. Kaylee Montgomery is a wonderful example. On November 8, 2024, during the state cross-country championship, the final race of her high school career, Kaylee was within sight of her goal: a personal best and a potential college scholarship. Yet, just 40 meters from the finish line, she saw a rival runner collapse. In that decisive moment, she set aside her ambitions, lifted her competitor's arm over her shoulders and helped her across the finish line. In that simple but powerful act, Kaylee demonstrated that humility is not weakness or a lack of ambition; it is strength expressed through compassion.

Humility also plays an essential role in personal growth. It opens us to feedback and makes us willing to learn from our mistakes. By embracing humility, we build resilience and adaptability, qualities vital for navigating life's inevitable challenges.

The myth that humility equates to weakness is rooted in societal norms that prioritize individual achievement over collective success. In reality, humility is a catalyst for collaboration and relationship-building. When we value the perspectives of others and recognize their contributions, we create environments where everyone feels seen, heard, and valued. Such inclusive cultures foster innovation and strengthen connections.

These truths come to life in the story of Mikaila Ulmer, a young entrepreneur who built a thriving business by prioritizing collaboration over competition. At just four and a half years old, Mikaila began selling lemonade made from her great-grandmother's 1940s recipe—sweetened with honey and driven by a mission to protect bees. What started as a neighborhood stand evolved into *Me & the Bees Lemonade*, now sold in over 1,500 stores nationwide.

Mikaila's journey is a powerful example of humble leadership. She consistently credits her team and community rather than seeking the spotlight for herself. Her commitment to social impact—donating a portion of profits to bee conservation—reveals a purpose that goes far beyond personal success. By choosing authenticity over self-promotion and collaboration over competition, she has built a brand grounded in integrity, trust, and meaningful influence.

Stories like these remind us that humility is not about shrinking into the shadows. It is about shining a light on others. Humility challenges us to redefine success, measuring it by collective achievement rather than individual accolades. It gives us the confidence to embrace our strengths while remaining open to growth and change.

Some also believe that humility equates to low self-esteem. This couldn't be further from the truth. Humility doesn't mean you think less of yourself; it's about thinking of others and fostering a balanced self-awareness. It's the grounded assurance that comes from knowing your worth without feeling the need to constantly advertise it. While low self-esteem can cripple personal growth, humility actually fuels it by encouraging us to recognize our strengths and limitations alike. This recognition is a powerful motivator for self-improvement, pushing us to become better without feeling inadequate.

Another prevalent myth is that humility implies passivity. In the competitive environments we navigate daily, it's easy to assume that being humble means stepping back or letting others take charge. However, humility is not about being passive. It's an active quality that fosters collaboration and open communication. Imagine a workplace where every team member feels valued and heard. Humility makes this possible by encouraging assertive yet respectful dialogue. When leaders communicate with humility, they don't shy away from difficult conversations. Instead, they approach them with empathy, listening more than they speak, and valuing input from all corners. This dynamic creates an atmosphere where innovation can flourish, as everyone feels empowered to contribute their ideas.

These examples show how humility transcends misconceptions, proving that it is not about fading into the background but about standing firmly with grace and intention. It is about being confident enough in oneself to acknowledge others' strengths without feeling threatened. Humility invites us to engage with the world openly, recognizing that there is always more to learn and room to grow.

Embracing humility requires courage and vulnerability, but it leads to profound personal and professional transformation. It is the foundation for strong relationships and meaningful contributions. As we navigate the complexities of modern life, humility offers a path toward deeper understanding, greater empathy, and authentic connection.

Transformation Prompt – 7 (Rest) and 1 (Prayer/Meditation)

• After pondering these misconceptions and myths surrounding humility, take some time in stillness and solitude to reflect on how they have impacted you. Then express your observations through prayer and meditation. Explore how embracing humility might enhance your interactions, personal growth, and overall well-being. By dispelling these myths and embracing humility's true nature, we unlock its transformative potential, enriching our lives and those around us.

In closing this exploration of humility's misunderstood nature, remember that this virtue isn't about losing oneself, but finding strength in serving others with sincerity and openness. Through humility, we discover a path not only towards personal fulfillment but also towards creating a more compassionate and connected world.

The Roots of Humility: Historical and Cultural Perspectives

Humility has deep roots stretching across diverse cultural and historical landscapes. Ancient Greek philosophy, a bedrock of Western thought, offers a fascinating insight into humility's early value. Philosophers like Socrates and Plato valued humility not as a self-deprecating trait but as an acknowledgment of one's limitations. They believed true wisdom stemmed from recognizing the vastness of what one does not know. This perspective positions humility as a foundation for learning and personal development, an idea that remains relevant in modern discourse. It's intriguing to consider how these ancient thinkers laid the groundwork for the concept of humility as we understand it today.

In contrast, Eastern philosophies approach humility with an emphasis on interconnectedness and harmony. Buddhism, for instance, teaches that humility arises from understanding our place within the greater whole. This view encourages letting go of ego-driven desires to achieve inner peace and balance. Similarly, Confucianism emphasizes humility as a social virtue, fostering respect and harmony within communities. These teachings highlight humility's role in creating cohesive societies where individual desires are balanced with collective well-being.

Cultural interpretations of humility vary widely across the globe. In many African cultures, the philosophy of ubuntu beautifully illustrates humility through the lens of communal identity. Ubuntu, often translated as "I am because we are," centers on the belief that our humanity is inextricably tied to the humanity of others. It encourages individuals to recognize their dependence on and responsibility to the broader community. Ubuntu fosters humility by reminding people that no one thrives in isolation and that dignity, respect, and compassion should guide our interactions with one another. This worldview promotes a form of humility rooted not in self-effacement, but in deep awareness of one's place within a larger, interconnected human family.

In Japan, the concept of 'kenjō' embodies modesty and respect for others. It manifests in everyday interactions, from bowing to avoid eye contact to speaking softly in public. 'Kenjō' reflects a deeply ingrained cultural value that prioritizes community harmony over individual assertion.

Meanwhile, Native American cultures often view humility as an integral part of community life. Many tribes believe that true strength lies in serving others and maintaining balance with nature. This perspective underscores humility's role in creating resilient communities that thrive on mutual support and respect.

The evolution of humility over time paints a fascinating picture of shifting societal values. During the Renaissance, a period marked by individualism and human achievement, humility experienced a decline in emphasis. Yet, even amidst this focus on personal glory, humility found a place in religious teachings that urged moderation and self-awareness.

One of the most profound examples of humility comes from the life of Jesus Christ. Despite His divine nature, Jesus consistently chose the path of service and self-sacrifice. He washed the feet of His disciples, associated with the marginalized, and ultimately gave His life for the sake of others. His humility was not a sign of weakness but a deliberate strength that redefined greatness as serving rather than being served. Through His actions, Jesus modeled a radical form of leadership, one grounded in compassion, selflessness, and deep respect for the dignity of every person. His example continues to inspire countless individuals and communities worldwide to pursue humility as a transformative force for both personal growth and collective well-being.

Stories from diverse cultures illustrate humility's universal appeal across time and space. Folktales often feature protagonists whose humble nature leads to unexpected triumphs. These narratives teach that humility is not about diminishing oneself but embracing one's humanity and imperfections. Cultural proverbs echo this sentiment, offering timeless wisdom on the value of remaining grounded and open to learning.

Consider the African proverb: "The higher the monkey climbs, the more it shows its tail." This saying reminds us that pride often precedes a fall, while humility keeps us grounded and wise. Similarly, the Chinese proverb "The man who removes a mountain begins by carrying away small stones" speaks to the power of patient humility in achieving great feats.

Humility's historical and cultural roots reveal its enduring significance across different eras and societies. Whether through ancient philosophy or cultural narratives, humility emerges as a timeless virtue that transcends cultural boundaries. It encourages us to embrace our limitations while remaining open to growth and connection with others.

In examining these varied perspectives, we see that humility is not a singular concept but a rich tapestry woven from diverse threads of human experience. It challenges us to reflect on our values and consider how we can integrate humility into our lives meaningfully.

Exploring these historical and cultural dimensions enriches our understanding of humility's place in contemporary society. By appreciating its roots, we gain insight into how this virtue has shaped human behavior throughout history and continues to do so today.

Transformation Prompt – 4 (Community) and 6 (Affirmations)

- Think about how your cultural background influences your understanding of humility. Did you grow up in a culture that emphasized individualism or valued connection? How has that shaped your worldview and self-worth?

- Reflect on any proverbs, parables, or stories that highlight humility's importance. Discuss with others how these narratives shape their perspective on what it means to be humble in today's world. Make note of the truths and beliefs you will continue reinforcing.

Humility and Confidence: Finding the Balance

Humility and confidence coexist in a dance that seems paradoxical at first glance. Yet, when one examines the essence of each, it becomes clear how they enhance one another. Humility isn't about shrinking away from one's abilities or achievements. Rather, it's about acknowledging them without letting them cloud our judgments or interactions. Confidence, then, steps in as the voice that reassures us of our value and capability, without tipping into arrogance. Think of confidence as a steady flame, bright enough to illuminate your path but not so intense that it blinds those around you. When humility tempers confidence, it creates a strong yet approachable presence that draws people in.

Consider Beth Ford, President and CEO of Land O'Lakes, Inc., who exemplifies a rare combination of humility and confident leadership at the helm of a major agribusiness and food cooperative. She is celebrated not only for her sharp business acumen but also for her grounded, approachable leadership style. Despite leading one of the largest farmer- and member-owned cooperatives in the United States, Ford consistently emphasizes the importance of enabling others' success over personal accolades. She openly acknowledges the value of collaboration and the strength that comes from listening to her team, fostering an environment where ideas are freely shared and innovation thrives.

Ford's leadership philosophy is captured well in her own words:

> *"You want to have humility, but you can't be shy to make clear to your supervisors, your leaders, whomever, what your aspiration is. Otherwise, people are going to just guess. Nobody, I promise you, cares more about your career than you do. And you have to remind yourself of that and do what you need to do to position yourself. To me, that means you enable others' success and then you'd be surprised that kinda it's a virtuous circle. Everybody wants to have you part of the team when you care legitimately about somebody else."*

Since becoming CEO in 2018, Ford has been recognized as one of Fortune's "Most Powerful Women" multiple times. Her confidence does not stem from projecting infallibility but from empowering her team and being honest about challenges, which has only strengthened her credibility and impact. Through this blend of humility and decisiveness, Ford has led Land O'Lakes to greater resilience and relevance in an ever-evolving industry, all while championing diversity, rural connectivity, and sustainable agriculture.

Other public figures and contemporary business leaders provide tangible examples of this balance in action. Mahatma Gandhi's life exemplifies humility intertwined with confident leadership. His quiet resolve and unwavering belief in non-violence led a nation to freedom without resorting to aggression. Satya Nadella, CEO of Microsoft, is renowned for steering the company with a focus on empathy and collaboration. His leadership style is built on listening and learning, qualities that amplify his confidence and effectiveness.

Dr. Martin Luther King, Jr. is another great example of humility combined with confident leadership. He led with deep moral conviction and an unshakable belief in justice, yet always carried himself with humility and grace. Dr. King's strength lay not in domination but in his ability to unite people around a shared vision of equality and hope. He acknowledged the enormity of the challenges faced, yet his speeches and actions conveyed a calm confidence that inspired millions to believe in the possibility of change. By embodying servant leadership, placing the needs of others above his own ambitions, he mobilized a movement that reshaped history. His legacy reminds us that true leadership is not about personal power but about elevating others and courageously pursuing a higher purpose.

However, maintaining this equilibrium isn't without its challenges. Facing criticism can be daunting, especially when it feels personal or unjustified. Here, humility offers perspective, allowing you to separate constructive feedback from emotional reactions. It encourages you to view criticism as an opportunity for growth rather than a personal affront. Strategies for maintaining self-esteem amidst criticism include practicing self-compassion and seeking supportive feedback from trusted colleagues or mentors.

In moments when self-doubt creeps in, remember that humility doesn't mean downplaying your achievements or strengths. It's about recognizing them while understanding that there's always room for growth and learning. Building confidence involves celebrating small victories and acknowledging progress, no matter how minor it may seem.

In professional settings, striking a balance between humility and assertiveness requires intentional effort. It's easy to fall into the trap of thinking that speaking up for oneself is incompatible with being humble.

**Yet, humility doesn't demand silence;
it calls for thoughtful expression.**

When presenting ideas or advocating for change, let your humility guide your tone and approach while allowing your confidence to assert your perspective firmly.

Finding harmony between humility and confidence allows you to build meaningful connections and inspire those around you. It is through this balance that we become more than just individuals striving for personal success; we become catalysts for positive change in our communities and beyond.

Realizing this delicate balance requires continuous practice and reflection. As you navigate through various roles in life—be it as a parent, partner, leader, or friend—observe how humility and confidence manifest in each context. Pay attention to how they influence your interactions and decisions. You'll find that when these traits work in tandem, they create a powerful synergy that transforms relationships and amplifies personal growth.

Transformation Prompt – 3 (Habit Tracking) and 6 (Community)

- Set aside time each week to jot down moments where you felt challenged or accomplished. Reflect on these experiences, noting where humility played a role and how confidence supported you. This practice not only sharpens self-awareness but also reinforces the interplay between these traits.

- Picture a scenario where you receive unexpected criticism at work. In this safe space, practice responding with humility by acknowledging the critique and expressing gratitude for the feedback. Then, engage your confidence by asserting your commitment to improvement and your belief in your skills. This exercise strengthens your ability to handle real-world situations with grace and assurance.

The Psychology of Humility: Understanding the Mindset

Researchers have identified humility as a catalyst for psychological resilience, empowering us to face life's uncertainties with courage and composure. When adversity strikes, humility equips us with the flexibility to adapt and grow. By embracing humility, we remain open to learning from setbacks and adjusting our course, which in turn strengthens our capacity to recover from difficulties and emerge stronger than before.

**Humility is a cornerstone of mental well-being,
quietly weaving resilience into the complex
fabric of our daily lives, much like an
unseen but ever-present thread.**

When we embrace humility, there is a noticeable reduction in both anxiety and stress, two formidable adversaries. It acts as a comforting, stabilizing force, reminding us that life's burdens do not have to become solitary struggles. By acknowledging our limitations, we open ourselves to a world of support and collaboration, thereby relieving the self-imposed pressure to achieve perfection. This acceptance of our imperfection fosters a profound sense of peace and serenity, allowing us to navigate life's inevitable challenges with a calm mind and a steady heart.

Humility plays a crucial role in enhancing empathy, a vital ingredient for establishing and maintaining meaningful connections. When we're humble, we have a natural tendency to listen more than we speak, attuning ourselves to the nuanced emotions and lived experiences of others. This heightened awareness and consideration for others' perspectives deepen our understanding and subsequently strengthen our relationships, building a foundation for mutual respect and shared growth.

From a cognitive perspective, humility profoundly influences how we process information and engage with the broader world around us. It encourages open-mindedness, breaking down the mental barriers that often confine us to rigid thinking patterns. By willingly accepting and acknowledging that we don't have all the answers, we remain endlessly receptive to new ideas and diverse perspectives, fostering a culture of continual learning and growth, both personally and collectively.

Humility also sharpens our listening skills considerably. When we're genuinely humble, we listen with the intent not merely to reply, but to understand, fully engaging with the essence of what others truly have to express. This gentle approach enhances our ability to communicate effectively and construct restorative bridges across apparent differences and divides.

Developing and nurturing a humble mindset requires an intentional practice intertwined with self-awareness. Mindfulness serves as a powerful tool in this transformative journey towards humility. By consciously staying present in each moment, we cultivate an awareness of our thoughts and emotions without the tarnishing hue of judgment. This delicate practice helps us gracefully recognize when our ego attempts to assume control, allowing us to respond with the traits of humility and grace.

Techniques for overcoming ingrained cognitive biases are also invaluable in this process. By challenging our long-held assumptions and questioning our entrenched beliefs, we create expansive space for humility to flourish. This thoughtful process involves examining our thoughts with a critical lens, seeking constructive feedback from others around us, and being wholeheartedly willing to change our perspectives when presented with new, compelling information. Over time, these practices contribute to the creation of a more humble, open, and receptive mindset.

Transformation Prompt – 1 (Prayer), 3 (Habit Tracking), and 4 (Community)

- Begin each morning this week with a simple prayer, asking for the strength to meet adversity with humility and openness. Ask God to help you release the pressure to appear perfect and instead embrace peace through honest dependence on Him and the support of others. Let your prayer be a grounding moment to center your heart on trust, not control.

- Choose three of the following acts of humility to track: listened with genuine intent, acknowledged a personal limitation without shame, asked for help or feedback, practiced open-mindedness in a difficult moment, responded to stress with grace instead of ego.

- Reach out to a trusted friend, mentor, or group and share one recent situation where humility helped you navigate a challenge or where you wish it had. Invite others to reflect with you, offer feedback, or even walk with you in tracking habits. Humility thrives in community, not isolation.

Humility and Emotional Intelligence: A Path to Self-awareness and Connection

Humility is intricately linked with emotional intelligence, regarded by many as a key component of both personal and professional success. Self-regulation, one of the foundational pillars of emotional intelligence, is deeply rooted within the tenets of humility. When we're humble, we're better equipped and more apt to manage our emotions, responding thoughtfully rather than reacting impulsively. This self-discipline and control grant us the ability to maintain composure amidst challenging situations, fostering a sense of stability, resilience, and inner strength.

Empathy, another critical aspect of emotional intelligence, thrives abundantly in the fertile ground of humility. By mindfully placing ourselves in others' shoes, we gain invaluable insight into their feelings, experiences, and motivations, subsequently building trust through shared understanding and rapport.

Erin Gruwell, the teacher behind the *Freedom Writers* movement, gives an illuminating example. Despite facing significant challenges with her at-risk students, Gruwell remained admirably humble, never assuming she knew everything. She chose to listen deeply to her students' stories, recognizing that their lived experiences were profound teachers in themselves. Her humility fostered an open and collaborative classroom environment where students felt valued and genuinely heard. This mutual respect and openness not only enhanced learning outcomes but also transformed her classroom into a supportive community where everyone, educators and learners alike, could thrive. As a result of her efforts, every one of her 150 students, many of whom had been written off by the system, graduated from high school, with many going on to attend college, breaking cycles of poverty and despair.

Humility is a journey worth taking, a path that leads not only to personal growth but to a deeper connection with the world around you. As you continue reading, I encourage you to keep an open mind and allow yourself to be transformed by the simple yet profound power of humility.

Humility is the mother of all virtues;
where there is humility, there is strength.

Akan Proverb

Chapter 2:

Everyday Acts of Humility

magine walking into a bustling café, where the aroma of fresh coffee mingles with the sound of lively chatter. As you approach the door, you notice an older woman struggling with her bags. You pause, reach out, and hold the door open for her. Can you imagine how much difference you've made in that woman's life? This simple act, seemingly small in the grand scheme of things, has made that person's life easier in that moment. That is humility. It's not about seeking recognition but about acknowledging the shared human experience. Every day actions like this ripple through our communities, touching lives in ways we might never fully grasp.

Offering help without waiting to be asked demonstrates attentiveness to others' needs. Whether it's assisting a coworker swamped with tasks or lending an ear to a friend in distress, these gestures of humility strengthen bonds and build community.

Being mindfully present transforms how we engage with the world. Picture a conversation where you truly listen to the other person without planning your response or interrupting. This presence signifies respect and understanding, qualities that nurture humility. When someone feels heard, they feel valued.

Humility often shines brightest in these ordinary moments. When you acknowledge a mistake in front of colleagues, it might seem daunting at first, but it builds trust and authenticity. Admitting "I was wrong" or "I don't know" doesn't diminish your competence; it enhances your credibility and openness. Mistakes become opportunities for growth and learning rather than sources of shame. By embracing vulnerability, you pave the way for deeper connections and mutual respect.

Part of humility is creating environments where everyone feels valued, but this requires intentional effort. Avoid using hierarchical language that places one person above another. Instead, focus on fostering equality and respect. Engage with people from diverse backgrounds and experiences; it enriches your perspective and deepens your understanding of humanity's vast tapestry. When you treat everyone with equal regard, you cultivate an atmosphere where humility thrives, and innovation blossoms.

Another opportunity for practicing humility is in routine tasks. In a meeting, share credit when discussing successful projects. Acknowledge the contributions of your team members, recognizing that success is rarely a solo achievement.

Ask for feedback and act on it. This openness not only fosters personal growth but also invites others to share their insights generously. Embracing feedback isn't about self-criticism; it's about continuous improvement and collaboration.

These are all ways we can show humility in our world today. But while it's great to practice humility in public, being humble at home, with the people who know us best, is just as important, if not more so. True humility is most meaningful when it's lived out in our closest relationships. Practicing humility at home creates an atmosphere of mutual respect, where love can deepen and everyone feels seen, heard, and valued. Apologizing sincerely when we've hurt someone, even if they're a child, models accountability and respect. It means listening with patience during disagreements and valuing others' perspectives, regardless of age or role. Sharing household responsibilities without keeping score, expressing gratitude for the little things, and being willing to ask for help all reflect a humility that nurtures trust and connection.

Incorporating humility into daily life doesn't require grand gestures. It thrives in simplicity, in the quiet moments when you choose kindness over self-interest, patience over impatience. As you go about your day, remember that every interaction holds the potential for humility to flourish. Embrace these moments as they come, knowing that each act, no matter how small, contributes to a more compassionate world.

Transformation Prompts – 2 (Journaling) and 3 (Habit Tracking)

- Think back to a time when someone acknowledged your efforts or listened without interruption. How did that make you feel?

- Reflect on how you can incorporate these acts of humility into your daily routine. Write them in a journal. Then, keep track of moments when you actually do them and note the results. This practice helps reinforce the value of these small actions and encourages mindful engagement in your interactions.

Navigating Humility in Social Media:
A Mindful Approach to Sharing and Connection

In the world of social media, maintaining humility can feel like navigating a minefield. Our feeds are filled with highlight reels, each post a carefully curated snapshot of success. It's tempting to fall into the trap of self-promotion, driven by the need for likes and shares. But this pressure can overshadow the authentic connections we crave. The challenge is real: how do we engage online without letting our ego take the wheel?

Awareness is the first step to change. Begin by analyzing your social media habits. Notice when you're scrolling out of boredom or seeking validation.. When you catch yourself mindlessly scrolling, pause and ask: *"What do I actually need right now?"* Connection? Rest? Inspiration? Redirect your attention with purpose. Reach out to a friend, journal a quick thought, or step outside for a breath of fresh air. These small shifts deepen your self-awareness and allow humility to guide how you engage with the world, even online.

Next is intentionality. Crafting an authentic online persona requires intentionality. Share content that reflects your true self, not just the shiny parts. Celebrate others' successes and engage with their stories genuinely. When commenting, aim for positivity and encouragement. These interactions build a community rooted in support rather than competition.

Conscious content creation means sharing with purpose. Before hitting "post," ask yourself: Does this contribute positively? Does it foster connection or understanding? Focus on content that builds bridges, not walls. Share stories that inspire, educate, or bring joy. Highlight issues that matter to you and invite others into meaningful conversation. This mindful approach transforms social media into a platform of community and collaboration. Remember, every post is a chance to uplift, not just showcase.

The practice of digital humility also involves embracing imperfection. We often present polished versions of ourselves online, but showing our humanity can be more powerful. Share lessons learned from failures or challenges overcome; these stories resonate deeply because they reflect reality. Authenticity invites empathy, allowing others to see themselves in your experiences. It fosters connections built on truth rather than illusion.

Reflecting on your digital presence also involves considering how it aligns with your values. Is your online presence consistent with who you are offline? Does it reflect humility, kindness, and respect? Periodically evaluate your online interactions and content through this lens. If something feels off, don't hesitate to adjust your approach. Authenticity requires ongoing reflection and adaptation as you grow and change.

Engaging with technology humbly means being a conscious consumer of content too. Follow creators who inspire thoughtful dialogue and contribute to your growth. Seek out diverse perspectives and engage respectfully with those who hold opposing views. This openness enriches your understanding and broadens your horizons.

Lastly, know when to go on a digital detox. Taking breaks from technology might seem daunting, but the benefits are profound. Scheduled digital detox days offer a reset for the mind and soul. Without constant notifications and updates, you have space to reconnect with what truly matters. Maybe it's spending time in nature, diving into a book, or sharing a meal with loved ones; these moments ground us in reality and remind us of life beyond screens. Plan these detoxes like you would any other important activity; mark them on your calendar and honor them.

By navigating social media and technology with humility, you contribute positively to the digital landscape. These platforms hold immense potential for connection and learning when approached mindfully. As you continue exploring ways to cultivate humility in daily life, remember that each interaction, whether in person or online, is an opportunity to practice this transformative virtue.

Living with Intention:
Making Humility a Daily Habit

You've already taken meaningful steps in Chapter One by engaging with the seven transformative tools introduced in this book, each one a seed planted on your journey toward greater humility. Now, I invite you to go deeper as we expand on the tools, explore new insights, incorporate powerful practices, and assimilate soul-stirring reflections designed to help you embody humility in ways that transform not just your inner world, but the lives around you. This is more than a continuation; it's an invitation to rise, to shine, and to become all you were created to be as you contribute to making the world a better place.

Starting each day with intention sets the tone for everything that follows. Imagine waking up and taking a moment to breathe deeply, centering yourself before the rush begins. This is your time to set a humility-focused intention. Think about incorporating morning affirmations that remind you of the humble path you want to walk. "I will approach today with openness and grace," or "I choose humility over pride." These affirmations aren't just words; they're commitments to live each day purposefully, aligning actions with values.

Setting daily humility goals further solidifies this intention. They don't have to be grandiose; simple goals like offering genuine praise or listening more can be transformative.

Throughout the day, conscious decision-making is your compass. When decisions arise, pause and consider the humble choice. Choosing collaboration over competition may mean inviting a colleague to join a project rather than going solo for the spotlight. Prioritizing service over self-interest could involve volunteering time to help a neighbor instead of binge-watching your favorite series. These choices define who you are and how you impact those around you. They create ripples of kindness and connection, proving that humility isn't passive; it's active and intentional.

Forming lasting habits around humility requires dedication and support. Habit tracking can be a game-changer, allowing you to monitor progress and stay accountable. Tracking these moments reinforces them, making humility second nature. Partnering with someone for accountability can also boost your efforts. Share your goals and check in regularly, celebrating successes and supporting each other through setbacks. This shared journey strengthens bonds and keeps you focused. Sharing milestones with a community, whether a small group of friends or an online forum, creates a sense of camaraderie. Celebrate the progress together, knowing every step forward is significant.

Most importantly, consistency is key, and celebrating it keeps motivation high. Weekly reviews of your humility practices provide an opportunity to reflect on what's working and where adjustments may be needed. Did you meet your goals? What challenges did you face? This reflection helps refine your approach and deepens your understanding of humility's role in your life.

Living with intention is not about perfection; it's about commitment.

It's recognizing that every day offers new opportunities to embrace humility in ways that enrich your life and those around you. It means actively choosing humility in moments big and small, knowing these choices shape your character and influence the world. As you integrate intentional living into your routine, you'll find that humility becomes more than just an abstract concept; it becomes an integral part of your daily existence, guiding you toward deeper connections and a more meaningful life.

Humility isn't about grand gestures; it's about the choices we make each day. It's found in the morning as you set your intentions, in the quiet moments when you choose service over self-interest, and in the consistent practice of reflecting on your growth. It's celebrated in shared milestones and accountability partnerships that keep you grounded and motivated. Living with intention means embracing humility as a daily habit, not just when convenient but as a guiding principle that shapes who you are. This commitment transforms ordinary days into extraordinary opportunities for growth and connection.

Practical Exercises:
Cultivating Humility through Mindful Actions

- Mindfulness and humility go hand in hand, offering a transformative way to navigate life. One simple yet profound practice is the "Humility Walk." Start by taking a stroll through your neighborhood or a local park. As you walk, focus on observing those around you. Notice the small acts of kindness, the shared smiles, and the moments of connection. This isn't about judging or comparing; it's about appreciating the myriad ways people interact. Let your observations inspire gratitude and reflection on how you can incorporate similar humility into your daily actions. It's a gentle reminder of the beauty in everyday kindness.

- Incorporating mindful breathing with humility affirmations can ground you in the present moment. Find a quiet spot, close your eyes, and take a deep breath in. As you exhale, silently repeat affirmations like "I am open to learning" or "I choose to listen first." These simple phrases can anchor you in humility, reinforcing a mindset of openness and acceptance. Regularly practicing this exercise can help you respond to challenges with grace and understanding, shifting your focus from ego to empathy.

- Role-playing scenarios offer another powerful tool for cultivating humility. Gather a few friends or colleagues and create situations where humility might be challenged. Practice responding to criticism with grace, focusing on listening rather than defending. In leadership settings, role-play scenarios where you must make decisions that prioritize the team's success over personal recognition. These exercises enhance your ability to navigate real-life situations with humility and composure, preparing you for moments when humility is tested.

- Visualization techniques are equally effective in reinforcing humble intentions. Before entering a significant meeting or social event, take a few minutes to visualize yourself interacting with humility. Picture yourself listening attentively, valuing others' contributions, and responding thoughtfully. Imagine successful, humble outcomes, where your choices lead to positive connections and constructive dialogue. Visualization strengthens your resolve to act with humility, creating a mental blueprint for success.

- Regular sessions of prayer and meditation focusing on humility can deepen your practice over time. Guided prayers and meditations on humility invite you to explore this virtue more deeply, fostering a sense of peace and balance. During these sessions, allow your thoughts to settle as you focus on your breath, welcoming feelings of gratitude and compassion. Mindful journaling exercises complement this practice by providing space for reflection on your experiences with humility. Write about moments when you felt humbled or witnessed humility in others. Journaling can capture insights and lessons learned, creating a personal record of growth.

Integrating these exercises into your routine doesn't require significant time commitments, yet it yields profound benefits. Each practice offers unique insights into how humility can manifest in your life, enhancing self-awareness and enriching interactions. Whether through mindful walks, breathing exercises, role-playing scenarios, visualization techniques, or prayer sessions, these mindful actions cultivate a deeper understanding of the power of humility.

Consider incorporating these practices into your daily routine, even if just for a few minutes each day. Over time, they'll become second nature, guiding you toward more humble interactions and genuine connections with others. Embrace these exercises as opportunities for growth, knowing that each step taken toward humility fosters a more compassionate and interconnected world.

As you engage with these practical exercises, remember that humility isn't about perfection or impressive feats. It's about the small choices made consistently, the quiet moments of reflection and learning. It's about recognizing our shared humanity and finding strength in serving others with sincerity and openness. By cultivating humility through mindful actions, you contribute to a world where empathy and understanding reign supreme, a world where humility lights the path to deeper connections and lasting fulfillment.

Humility in Conversation: Listening and Responding with Grace

Engaging in conversation is an art, and humility serves as its canvas. Imagine sitting across from someone, fully present and engaged. Active listening becomes your brush, painting a picture of empathy and respect. It's about more than just hearing words; it's about truly understanding the other person. Effective listening involves being fully present, paying attention to verbal and nonverbal cues, avoiding distractions, and demonstrating understanding through questions and summaries. When you allow someone to finish their thoughts without interruption, you create a space where they feel valued and important.

Good listening doesn't just enhance conversations; it deepens relationships.

Responding with grace involves another layer of humility. When you engage with others, use empathetic language that acknowledges their feelings and perspectives. Simple phrases like "I understand where you're coming from" or "That sounds challenging" validate their experiences. This approach shifts the focus from defending your point to appreciating theirs. Be grateful they are willing to share their thoughts, ideas, beliefs, and emotions with you. Create a safe place that is free of judgment. Such acknowledgment doesn't mean you agree with everything; it signals respect for their viewpoint. It's a subtle yet powerful way to build bridges and foster mutual trust.

Practicing conversational humility, especially in debates, means choosing wisdom over winning. It's a recognition that meaningful dialogue isn't about defeating another viewpoint, but about allowing multiple perspectives to refine and elevate collective clarity. When discussions become heated, asking open-ended questions can transform the dynamic. Questions like "Can you tell me more about that?" or "How did you arrive at that conclusion?" invite the other person to share more deeply. These kinds of inquiries don't just diffuse tension, they create space for new insights to emerge, often revealing solutions neither side could have reached alone. By emphasizing curiosity and the pursuit of collective wisdom, you help keep conversations grounded in mutual trust and shared growth.

Humility also plays a crucial role in resolving conflicts. Conversations may become tense, emotions may run high, and words spoken in haste might create rifts. Here, humility acts as a balm. It starts with acknowledging your role in the conflict and expressing a genuine desire to find common ground. Finding common ground often requires setting aside ego and focusing on shared values. Instead of fixating on differences, look for areas of agreement or mutual interest. This shift in perspective invites collaboration rather than confrontation. When both parties feel heard and respected, solutions become more accessible. Humility encourages you to prioritize the relationship over being right, which can lead to more constructive discussions and reduced tension.

Consider the impact of humility in everyday interactions too. Whether chatting with a colleague or catching up with a friend, these principles apply universally. Approaching each conversation with an open mind and heart enriches your connections and deepens your understanding of those around you. This mindset fosters an environment where everyone feels empowered to share their thoughts openly.

Incorporating humility into conversations isn't about being passive or self-effacing. It's about engaging authentically, valuing others' input, and nurturing an atmosphere of trust and respect. Through active listening, empathetic responses, and a focus on understanding over winning, you create meaningful exchanges that uplift and inspire. By practicing conversational humility, you contribute positively to your relationships and communities, building connections that are both strong and enduring.

As you continue exploring ways to cultivate humility, remember that every conversation holds potential for growth and connection. Whether you're navigating a conflict or simply catching up with a friend, let humility guide your words and actions, paving the way for deeper understanding and lasting bonds.

Overcoming Ego:
Strategies for Humility in Challenging Situations

Navigating a stressful work environment or a competitive social setting often stirs up ego-driven responses that can overshadow humility. These situations trigger the ego's desire to shine, to be recognized, and to stand out. Recognizing these triggers is the first step in overcoming them. When you find yourself in a high-pressure meeting or a gathering where everyone seems to be one-upping each other, pause. Notice how your body reacts. Maybe your heart races or your mind starts crafting clever comebacks. This awareness starts you on the path to taking back control, allowing humility to guide your actions rather than ego.

Once you're aware of your body's reaction, you can then create and implement strategies to counteract ego and transform these challenging moments into opportunities for growth. Practicing self-compassion is a powerful tool in this arsenal. Instead of harsh self-criticism when things don't go your way, treat yourself with the same kindness you'd offer a friend in similar circumstances. This shift in perspective softens the ego's grip, making room for humility. Reframe competitive thoughts by focusing on collaboration rather than competition. When you see others as allies rather than rivals, you open yourself up to learning from their insights and experiences, enriching your own journey.

Value others' contributions, and in so doing, you cultivate an environment where humility thrives. Publicly acknowledging the efforts of your team or peers not only lifts them but reinforces your own humility. Imagine being in a meeting where credit is shared freely; not only does it foster camaraderie, but it also highlights the collective effort behind success.

Building resilience against ego requires regular reflection on humble values and developing a growth mindset. Reflecting on what humility means to you and how it manifests in your life grounds you in these values, even when ego tempts you to stray. This reflection doesn't have to be a lengthy process; even a few minutes of quiet contemplation can refocus your intentions. A growth mindset, which embraces challenges and sees failures as learning opportunities, further fortifies your resilience. When you view setbacks as stepping stones rather than stumbling blocks, humility guides you to persevere and adapt without letting ego derail your progress.

> **These practices aren't about denying your ego's existence but about understanding its role and learning to balance it with humility.**

The key lies in these small shifts—pausing to reflect before reacting, choosing collaboration over competition, and valuing the contributions of others. By nurturing these habits, you gradually transform challenging situations into opportunities for personal growth and deeper connections with those around you.

In today's fast-paced world, where pressure mounts and competition is fierce, maintaining humility is both an art and a discipline. It requires conscious effort and commitment to valuing humility over ego-driven desires. Each step you take toward humility, each moment of reflection or choice to uplift others, strengthens your resolve to live authentically and compassionately. As you navigate through work pressures and social dynamics, remember that humility isn't about diminishing yourself; it's about lifting others while staying true to who you are.

Gratitude and Humility: A Powerful Duo

Gratitude and humility form a symbiotic relationship, each enhancing the other in a subtle yet profound way. When you practice gratitude, you naturally shift your focus outward, acknowledging the actions and efforts of those around you. This act of recognition fosters humility by reminding you that your successes and joys are often built on the support and contributions of others. Consider starting a daily gratitude journal where you jot down simple things you're grateful for. It might be a kind word from a friend or a moment of laughter shared with family. These reflections keep your attention on the positive and cultivate a humble heart.

In conversations, expressing gratitude can transform interactions. When someone helps you out, a heartfelt "thank you" goes a long way in showing appreciation for their effort. It's a small gesture, but one that speaks volumes about your character.

Gratitude letters offer another layer of depth. Writing to mentors or individuals who've guided you not only strengthens bonds but also humbles you as you acknowledge their impact on your journey. These letters can be heartfelt and personal, making the recipient feel valued and appreciated.

Gratitude sharing circles are also an excellent way to practice communal gratitude. Gather with friends or family and take turns sharing what you're thankful for. This simple exercise builds connections and encourages humility by highlighting everyone's contributions to the group's well-being.

In family settings, acknowledging each member's contributions nurtures a sense of belonging and respect. Celebrate shared achievements, whether it's a successful team project at work or a family milestone like a graduation or anniversary. These celebrations remind everyone that success is sweeter when shared, reinforcing humility in the process.

Sustaining a gratitude mindset requires commitment but yields rewards that enrich your life deeply. Monthly gratitude reflection sessions offer an opportunity to look back at the month's highlights and express appreciation for the people and experiences that made it special. These reflections ground you in humility, reinforcing the interconnectedness of your life experiences.

Incorporating gratitude rituals before meals or bedtime instills a sense of peace and contentment. Before eating, pause to consider the effort that went into bringing food to your table. Thank God for His provision beyond the food that is directly in front of you. At bedtime, reflect on the day's positives, no matter how small they might seem. These rituals anchor you in humility, reminding you of life's abundance even amidst challenges.

As we close this chapter on cultivating humility in daily life, remember that humility isn't about heroic moments but small, intentional acts that weave together to form a humble existence. Gratitude plays a pivotal role in this process, transforming how we see ourselves and our place in the world. By focusing on what we have and those who support us, we nurture humility as a natural extension of gratitude.

In the next chapter, we'll explore how humility shapes truly influential leadership. Together, we'll examine how humble leadership creates space for collaboration, innovation, and meaningful influence—both in the workplace and beyond. Let's keep dancing forward as we discover how humility can elevate not just who we are, but how we lead.

Power is dangerous unless
you have humility.

Richard J. Daley

Chapter 3:

Humble Leadership

P icture a leader not known for commanding presence or thunderous speeches, but rather for a quiet strength that draws people in. This leader listens more than they speak, values collaboration over unilateral decisions, and measures success not by personal accolades but by collective achievements. This is the essence of humble leadership, a style that challenges traditional notions of authority by emphasizing humility as a core strength. Conventional leadership often conjures images of authoritarian figures who wield power with a firm hand, expecting compliance without question. In contrast, humble leaders thrive on empathy and understanding, creating environments that foster growth and innovation.

The impact of humble leadership on organizational culture is profound. It fosters an atmosphere where open communication is the norm rather than the exception. Humble leaders provide the psychological safety necessary for creativity to flourish, allowing employees to experiment and learn from failures without fear of judgment. Employees are encouraged to speak up, share ideas, and challenge the status quo without fear of retribution. This openness cultivates an innovative spirit, as teams are more willing to take calculated risks and explore unconventional solutions.

Humble leaders excel in creating spaces where ideas flow freely from all levels, not just top executives. Rather than dictating solutions, they facilitate discussions that encourage team input, resulting in well-rounded and inclusive decisions. This reduces blind spots, boosts engagement, and leads to more well-rounded outcomes.

To see humility in leadership in action, look no further than the late Herb Kelleher, co-founder of Southwest Airlines. Known for his unpretentious management style, Kelleher often prioritized people over profits, which created a culture of loyalty and satisfaction that translated into exceptional customer service. Kelleher's humility shone through in his willingness to engage with employees at all levels, from baggage handlers to pilots, ensuring everyone felt part of the company's success story.

Humble leaders like Kelleher prove that humility is not a weakness but a formidable strength in leadership. They demonstrate that influence is not about exerting authority but empowering others to reach their potential. By redefining traditional power structures, these leaders create environments where innovation thrives and mutual respect prevails. Through humility, they build organizations that are not only successful but also resilient and adaptable in the face of challenges.

Transformation Prompt – 2 (Journaling) and 1 (Prayer/Meditation)

- Think about a leader you admire who exemplifies humility. Reflect on specific actions they took that demonstrated humble leadership. How did these actions impact their team or organization positively? Write down your thoughts and observations in a journal to deepen your understanding of how humility shapes effective leadership. Spend time in prayer and meditation, pondering how those qualities can become a part of your leadership.

Servant Leadership: Empowering Others Through Humility

Servant leadership flips the traditional leadership model on its head by placing the needs of others at the forefront. At its core, it's about prioritizing the growth and well-being of your team over personal glory. This approach fosters a culture of humility, where leaders see themselves as part of the team rather than above it. The concept originated with Robert Greenleaf in the 1970s, who believed that true leadership begins with service. This philosophy encourages leaders to listen actively, empathize, and nurture their team members' talents. Instead of wielding power through authority, servant leaders empower others by creating an environment where everyone feels valued and heard.

The benefits of adopting servant leadership are numerous. Take Jacinda Ardern, former Prime Minister of New Zealand. Her leadership style was marked by empathy, humility, and a focus on collective well-being. During times of crisis, such as the Christchurch mosque shootings and the COVID-19 pandemic, Ardern consistently prioritized the needs of her people, communicated transparently, and led with compassion. Her approach fostered trust, unity, and a strong sense of social responsibility. Ardern's tenure demonstrates how servant leadership in politics can inspire national resilience and cultivate a culture grounded in care and collaboration.

In the workplace, we hear positive stories from employees under servant leaders. Employees often report feeling more connected to their work and colleagues, leading to a stronger commitment to their company's mission. Servant leadership fosters a sense of ownership and responsibility among team members, leading to a more dynamic and collaborative workplace. Empowered employees are more likely to innovate and push boundaries, knowing they have the backing of a leader who trusts them to succeed. When people feel respected and supported, they're more likely to be engaged and motivated at work. This engagement translates into higher productivity and creativity, as employees are encouraged to take initiative and bring their ideas to the table.

Companies like Salesforce, Costco, and The Ritz-Carlton stand out for their commitment to servant leadership and empowering their employees at every level. These organizations thrive by placing humility at the heart of their culture, prioritizing collaboration over ego and curiosity over control. In these environments, team members feel safe to share ideas without fear of judgment. Leaders don't position themselves as the sole source of wisdom; instead, they create space for innovation to flourish organically. By stepping back and letting others shine, they cultivate teams that are more creative, engaged, and ultimately more successful.

If you're looking to adopt servant leadership principles in your own interactions, start by focusing on active listening during team meetings. Encourage open dialogue and make it a point to solicit input from everyone, not just the most outspoken members. This can be as simple as going around the room or asking quieter team members for their thoughts. By giving everyone a voice, you foster an inclusive environment that values diverse perspectives.

Also consider encouraging team-led initiatives by allowing employees to take charge of projects that align with their strengths and interests. This empowerment not only boosts morale but also enhances individual growth and development.

Mentoring offers another avenue for you to practice servant leadership. Approach it with humility, recognizing that while you have knowledge to share, there's always something to learn from those you mentor.

The principles of servant leadership can transform how we approach authority and influence. By focusing on serving others first, we create environments where humility and empathy are the norm rather than the exception. This shift not only benefits employees but also strengthens organizations as a whole. Whether you're leading a small team or a large corporation, incorporating servant leadership into your style can yield remarkable results.

Transformation Prompt – 3 (Habit Tracking) and 6 (Affirmations)

- As you reflect on these ideas, consider how you might implement servant leadership in your own life. Think about specific ways you can prioritize the needs of others and create spaces where everyone feels valued and heard. Write three of these ways down on a habit tracking chart and practice them until they become natural.

- Write affirmations that will enable you to focus on implementing the new habits you have chosen.

By embracing this approach, you'll empower those around you and contribute to a high-impact culture of humility.

Humility in Decision-Making: Balancing Confidence with Modesty

In the fast-paced world of leadership, decision-making often feels like an intricate dance, requiring a delicate balance of confidence and modesty. Humility plays a crucial role in this process, guiding leaders to make thoughtful decisions by assessing risks and opportunities with a level-headed approach. Instead of rushing into choices driven by ego or pressure, humble leaders take a step back to consider how a decision will affect everyone. They weigh the potential outcomes more thoroughly, ensuring that decisions align with both short-term goals and long-term vision.

They seek diverse perspectives before arriving at conclusions. This inclusivity enriches the decision-making process by incorporating a wide range of insights, which can often reveal blind spots or new opportunities. By actively inviting input from team members, regardless of rank or experience, leaders cultivate an environment where collaboration thrives. This collective approach not only enhances the quality of decisions but also fosters a sense of ownership and accountability among team members.

Implementing a decision-review process is another effective technique for reinforcing humility in leadership. After a decision is made, taking the time to reflect on its outcomes and the process that led to it can yield valuable lessons. This reflection encourages ongoing learning and adaptation, allowing leaders to refine their approach over time. It also provides a platform for discussing what went well and what could be improved, fostering an atmosphere of continuous improvement.

The impact of humility on decision outcomes is evident in case studies where leaders have avoided pitfalls through humble deliberation. Consider a scenario where a company was contemplating a major product launch. Instead of pushing forward despite potential issues, the leadership team took a step back to re-evaluate based on feedback from various departments. This humility-driven pause allowed them to address concerns proactively, leading to a successful launch that avoided costly setbacks.

Challenges in maintaining humility during decision-making often stem from managing ego, especially when deeply personal issues are at stake. It's easy for leaders to become defensive when their ideas are challenged or when pride is on the line. However, recognizing these ego-driven impulses allows leaders to step back and approach decisions with a clearer, more objective mindset. Accountability and feedback play a vital role here. Humble leaders encourage open dialogue where feedback is not only welcomed but actively sought out. By creating an environment where constructive criticism is valued, leaders can keep ego in check and remain grounded in humility.

Humble decision-makers also recognize the importance of being accountable for their actions. This accountability extends beyond just accepting responsibility for outcomes; it involves being transparent with team members about decision-making processes and inviting them into the conversation. When leaders model this behavior, it sets a precedent for honesty and integrity throughout the organization.

Humility in leadership is not about diminishing one's confidence or authority; it's about complementing those strengths with modesty and openness to learning. Through humble decision-making, leaders create environments where collaboration flourishes, innovation thrives, and trust is built, laying the foundation for sustained success and growth in any endeavor.

Transformation Prompt – 4 (Community) and 7 (Rest)

- To overcome challenges in maintaining humility, it can be helpful for leaders to establish personal accountability partnerships. These partnerships involve regularly checking in with a trusted colleague or mentor who can provide honest feedback and support. Sharing experiences and discussing decisions openly can help leaders identify areas where ego may have influenced their choices and explore ways to enhance humility moving forward. Identify your accountability partner(s) and invite them to join you on this journey.

Most importantly, don't allow yourself to get weighed down on this journey. It does not all depend on you for growth to happen. Allow yourself to receive grace and strength from God, as well as support from others.

Building Trust:
The Role of Humility in Teams

When you think about trust within a team, humility may not be the first connection you that comes to mind. Yet, it serves as the bedrock for trust. Imagine a team where everyone feels heard and valued. That's the magic humility brings. It fosters open communication, creating a safe space where team members can share ideas without fear of judgment. This environment of trust starts when leaders admit they don't have all the answers and are open to learning from their team. This vulnerability doesn't undermine authority; it actually builds a bridge to genuine connections.

Trust-building isn't something that happens overnight, but there are actionable steps you can take. Start with transparency in leadership decisions. When you explain why certain choices are made, it demystifies the process and breeds trust. Regular team-building exercises that focus on fostering trust can also help. These activities aren't just about having fun; they're about understanding each other on a deeper level. When you see your colleagues as people rather than just coworkers, it changes the dynamic. It builds empathy and strengthens the bonds that hold the team together.

A trust-based team environment offers numerous benefits, enhancing performance and collaboration. Teams that trust each other innovate more because they aren't afraid to take calculated risks. This environment encourages creativity, where ideas flow freely without fear of criticism. This openness to experimentation leads to groundbreaking ideas and solutions. Companies like Google thrive on this principle. By maintaining a culture where every voice is heard and valued, Google has become synonymous with innovation. They understand that great ideas can come from anywhere, and it's the humble leaders who recognize and nurture this potential.

Trust also reduces conflict, as open communication allows issues to be addressed before they escalate. When team members feel secure, morale improves significantly, leading to a more positive workplace atmosphere.

One powerful example of trust-building through humility comes from Delta Air Lines under the leadership of CEO Ed Bastian. During the height of the COVID-19 crisis, Bastian took a 100% pay cut and publicly acknowledged the sacrifices employees were making. Rather than resorting to mass layoffs, Delta launched voluntary leave programs and maintained open, honest communication with staff at every level. Bastian also personally wrote regular updates and video messages to employees, inviting feedback and showing appreciation. This transparent and humble approach helped sustain trust, morale, and loyalty, even in the face of uncertainty. Employees reported feeling respected and seen, reinforcing a culture of mutual commitment and collaboration.

Another powerful example comes from Cleveland Clinic, where humble leadership helped transform a culture of employee dissatisfaction. Under the leadership of CEO Dr. Toby Cosgrove, the organization made a conscious effort to listen to frontline workers and improve its emotional and relational culture. After receiving low scores on empathy and communication in internal surveys, Cosgrove implemented system-wide initiatives such as monthly town halls, leadership rounding (where leaders regularly visit departments to listen to staff), and a renewed emphasis on patient and employee experience. Leaders not only solicited feedback, but they also acted on it. As a result, Cleveland Clinic saw improvements in employee engagement, communication, and patient satisfaction. This transformation illustrates how humility in leadership, especially in high-pressure fields like healthcare, can build trust, boost morale, and lead to lasting success.

Building trust through humility isn't just about improving workplace dynamics; it's about creating an environment where everyone thrives. When teams operate with trust at their core, they become more resilient and adaptable to change. They support each other through challenges and celebrate victories together. This collective strength becomes a competitive advantage in navigating the complexities of today's business landscape.

Incorporating humility into your leadership style is key to building trust within your team. It requires consistent effort and a genuine commitment to valuing others' contributions. As you foster an environment where humility leads the way, you'll find that trust becomes not just an aspiration, but a reality that transforms your team's effectiveness and cohesion.

Transformation Prompt – 5 (Gratitude) and 4 (Community)

- Take some time to notice and express gratitude for your own progress so far on this journey. If you are having difficulty seeing the ways humility has changed you, reach out to someone else and ask them to share their observations. It is sometimes easier for others to see our growth when we are in the middle of a challenging trek. You can also ask them about how you can integrate these principles into your own leadership approach. Consider ways you can enhance transparency, encourage open communication, and prioritize team-building activities focused on trust.

By embracing humility as a foundational element of your leadership style, you'll create a culture where trust flourishes and everyone feels empowered to contribute their best.

Navigating Power Dynamics: Humility in High-Stakes Environments

Power dynamics in leadership often resemble a complex chessboard, where each move can shift the balance. In high-stakes environments where pressure mounts and decisions carry significant weight, understanding these power structures is crucial. Power can subtly influence interactions, and without mindfulness, it may lead to unintended imbalances. Humility, however, serves as an anchor, guiding leaders through these turbulent waters. It allows them to recognize the influence they wield and use it responsibly. It ensures that leaders remain grounded and focused on the best interests of their teams and organizations rather than on personal gain. They not only enhance their effectiveness but also inspire those around them to do the same. By acknowledging the weight of their decisions, humble leaders mitigate power imbalances, creating a space where inclusivity thrives.

Practicing humility in negotiations is especially challenging but equally rewarding. It involves listening more than speaking and finding common ground rather than insisting on one's way. Imagine entering a negotiation room not as a battlefield but as a place for dialogue. Here, humility becomes the bridge that connects differing perspectives. It encourages mutual respect and understanding, laying the foundation for agreements that benefit all parties involved.

Balancing authority with accessibility is another vital aspect. Leaders who remain approachable despite their power foster trust and openness, dismantling barriers that often hinder genuine communication.

The impact of humility in power dynamics extends beyond individual interactions. It leads to more equitable and effective outcomes by fostering an environment where everyone's voice matters. In scenarios of conflict resolution, humility plays a pivotal role. Leaders who approach disputes with a willingness to understand rather than dominate tend to find solutions that are sustainable and just. Successful conflict resolution through humility isn't about winning or losing; it's about reaching a consensus that respects all involved. Imagine a world where not only business leaders, but also educational leaders and political leaders chose humility. Each of us plays a role in making that a reality.

Consider the story of Dr. Tiffany Anderson, a superintendent known for transforming struggling school districts through humility and inclusive leadership. When she took on the challenge of revitalizing Topeka Public Schools, a district facing significant disparities and resource constraints, she didn't impose top-down mandates. Instead, Dr. Anderson adopted a consultative approach: regularly visiting schools, listening to teachers, students, and families, and inviting their input in shaping district policies and improvement plans. She even rode school buses and helped clean cafeterias to better understand everyday experiences. This humility-driven strategy empowered stakeholders at every level, turning what could have been a difficult restructuring process into a collective opportunity for growth. Her leadership helped boost student performance, increase graduation rates, and rebuild trust within the community. That's the power of humility in conflict resolution.

Diplomatic negotiations offer another rich tapestry of examples where humility reshapes power dynamics. Imagine two nations at an impasse over trade agreements. Traditional approaches might involve posturing and ultimatums. However, when leaders step back and engage with humility, focusing on shared interests rather than individual gains, the tone shifts. This shift opens doors to creative solutions that might have been overlooked in more adverse settings.

Humble leaders need to implement strategies for maintaining humility amidst complex power dynamics to create equitable environments. One approach involves continuous self-reflection, acknowledging biases and striving for balance between confidence and modesty. Seeking feedback from peers and team members also grounds leaders, reminding them of the collective wisdom within their organization. This openness to feedback reinforces the idea that leadership is not a solitary endeavor but a collaborative effort.

Balancing authority with accessibility requires leaders to remain approachable, even when wielding significant influence. It's about creating an atmosphere where people feel comfortable sharing ideas and concerns without fear of retribution. Leaders who practice this balance cultivate trust and loyalty, fostering a culture of transparency.

In corporate settings, humility-driven leadership can redefine organizational hierarchies. Imagine a company undergoing significant change—perhaps restructuring or expansion into new markets. A leader who embraces humility during this process acknowledges the expertise and insights of employees across all levels, facilitating smoother transitions and fostering innovation. You can be that leader!

The power dynamics inherent in leadership roles need not be overwhelming or divisive. By embracing humility, leaders navigate these complexities with grace and integrity, creating environments where everyone thrives. Humility serves as both a compass and an anchor, guiding leaders through crucial situations while ensuring beneficial outcomes for all involved.

Humility as a Competitive Edge: A Smarter Way to Lead

In the hectic world of business, where everyone is jostling for the spotlight, humility can seem like a paradox. But here's the twist: humility is about showing up differently. It's the ability to allow situations to evolve in a way that you didn't plan. And in so doing, you open the possibility of those situations turning out better than you could have ever hoped. This is not just a personal virtue; it's a strategic advantage.

Humility also fosters authentic connections with customers, turning them from mere transaction parties into loyal advocates. When customers feel genuinely valued, not just as numbers on a ledger, they return and they bring others with them. This kind of authentic relationship-building is far more than good manners; it's smart business.

Consider how humility differentiates a brand. In a market flooded with flashy advertisements and loud claims, a humble approach can be refreshing. It builds trust. A brand that listens to its customers, acknowledges mistakes, and strives for improvement stands out. This differentiation isn't about being the loudest voice but the most sincere. Customers appreciate brands that admit they don't know everything and are willing to learn and adapt.

Leveraging humility competitively requires intentional strategies. Start by fostering collaborative partnerships with humility at the core. Approach potential partners with an openness to learn and grow together. This collaboration should be mutually beneficial, where both parties feel respected and valued. Additionally, implementing customer feedback loops is vital for continual improvement. Actively seek out customer opinions and act on them. This feedback loop not only enhances products and services but also strengthens customer loyalty.

Another strategy to stand out is to focus on long-term relationships rather than short-term gains. Building genuine connections with stakeholders, be it customers, partners, or employees, creates a foundation for sustainable success. Humble leaders view competition not as a winner-takes-all game, but as an opportunity for mutual growth and advancement.

For leaders looking to incorporate humility into their competitive strategy, it's important to lead by example.

Model humility in everyday interactions by openly acknowledging the contributions of others and celebrating team achievements over personal accolades. Foster a culture where curiosity is encouraged, questions are welcomed, and mistakes are embraced as valuable learning opportunities, not signs of weakness. Perhaps most importantly, don't shy away from offering a sincere apology when necessary; it demonstrates strength, builds trust, and reinforces a culture rooted in accountability and respect.

Incorporating humility into business isn't about downplaying achievements; it's about recognizing the collective effort behind them. It's about valuing every individual's input and creating an atmosphere where everyone feels empowered to contribute their best. When leaders embody these principles, they foster an organizational culture that stands out for all the right reasons.

By embracing humility as a competitive edge, businesses can differentiate themselves in meaningful ways. This approach not only builds stronger customer relationships but also drives innovation and growth within the organization. Ultimately, it's the humble leaders who create lasting impact, the ones who understand that true success comes from lifting others up and valuing their contributions to the bigger picture.

Leading with Empathy: How Humility Fosters Stronger Connections

Imagine a leader who doesn't just hear words but truly listens, absorbing the emotions and nuances behind each sentence. This is where empathy and humility intersect, creating a leadership style that's both powerful and gentle. Empathy enhances understanding, allowing leaders to connect deeply with their team. It's not just about knowing what your employees are saying, but feeling what they're experiencing.

When combined with humility, empathy transforms leadership into a platform for authentic connection and growth. This symbiotic relationship encourages leaders to step back, see through the eyes of others, and respond with genuine care.

Humble leaders don't just lead; they inspire.

Empathy plays a crucial role in the success of any leader. It lays the groundwork for stronger team dynamics and builds unwavering loyalty. When leaders approach situations with empathy, they foster an environment where employees feel valued and understood. This understanding leads to increased retention because people are more likely to stay where they feel appreciated and supported. Teams flourish when they know their leader is in tune with their needs and concerns. Empathetic leadership encourages open dialogue, where every voice is heard and respected. It's about creating a culture where empathy isn't just a word but a way of operating.

Leaders who exemplify empathy inspire those around them with their approachability and understanding. Consider Howard Schultz, former CEO of Starbucks, who consistently prioritized employee well-being. His empathetic leadership style paved the way for groundbreaking benefits like healthcare for part-time workers and college tuition assistance. Schultz's ability to connect with employees on a personal level fostered loyalty and commitment within the company. Testimonials from Starbucks employees often highlight how his empathetic approach made them feel valued and motivated to contribute their best.

To cultivate empathy within your team, practical exercises can make a significant difference. Role-playing scenarios focusing on empathetic responses are effective in honing this skill. Imagine a team meeting where members take turns sharing challenges they face, while others practice responding with empathy, seeking to understand rather than judge. These exercises build a foundation of trust and respect, strengthening bonds among team members. Empathy circles also provide an opportunity for sharing and listening. In these circles, participants share personal stories or challenges while the rest of the group listens without interrupting. This practice also reinforces the power of listening as a tool for connection.

Empathetic leadership isn't just about being nice; it's about understanding the deeper needs of your team and responding in ways that foster growth and unity. By embracing empathy alongside humility, leaders create environments where everyone feels important. This approach not only strengthens relationships within teams but also enhances overall organizational resilience.

As we wrap up this chapter on humility in leadership, remember that empathy is a powerful tool that complements humility beautifully. Together, they form a leadership style that prioritizes connection over command, understanding over authority.

The next chapter will explore humility's role in relationships beyond the workplace—how it can transform personal connections into sources of strength and support. With each step of this dance, humility leads us into more personal spaces, inviting us to move with intention and compassion in our relationships with family, friends, and neighbors.

True love is quiescent, except in the nascent moments of true humility.

Bryant H. McGill

Chapter 4:

Humility in Relationships

Picture a family sitting on a front porch as the sun sets: parents, children, siblings, and maybe even grandparents. There's a calm in the air, a quiet understanding among them. Words aren't always necessary in these moments. What connects them is something deeper: a spirit of humility that allows each person to show up as they are, flawed, growing, and still worthy of love.

In close relationships, whether between spouses, siblings, or parents and children, humility serves as the bridge that unites hearts. It means acknowledging we don't have all the answers, and being okay with that. It invites us to listen with empathy, to say "I was wrong" without defensiveness, and to prioritize connection over being right. This mindset fosters trust, softens tensions, and strengthens bonds that might otherwise fray under the pressures of daily life.

Humility nurtures openness. When we admit we don't always know best, we create space for others to speak, share, and be truly heard. Whether it's a spouse confiding their fears, a child explaining their feelings, or a sibling asking for grace, humility allows us to meet those moments without judgment. It's about genuinely caring for one another.

In family dynamics, effective communication depends on this posture. Imagine a parent listening to a teenager without jumping to conclusions, or two siblings resolving a disagreement without assigning blame. Humble conversations aren't just about compromise; they're about curiosity and compassion. They turn conflicts into growth and misunderstandings into deeper understanding.

When problems arise, be it household decisions, caregiving roles, or generational differences, humility encourages collaboration. Each person's perspective becomes part of a shared solution, and responsibilities are distributed with mutual respect. In this way, humility builds not just love, but a home rooted in grace, teamwork, and trust.

Real-life stories reflect this truth. Consider the experience of a parent who, after a moment of frustration, snapped at their child. Recognizing the mistake, they sit down with their child, apologize sincerely, and explain that even adults mess up. This act of humility not only mends the immediate hurt but also models accountability, teaching the child the importance of owning up to one's actions.

On the Siblings with a Mission website, a woman named Analia Rodriguez shares her journey growing up with her brother Eli, who has Down Syndrome and autism. Despite the challenges, Analia's unwavering support and love for Eli exemplify the profound bond siblings can share. She recalls the joy of hearing Eli say "I love Ana" for the first time after 15 years, a moment that underscored the depth of their connection. In every relationship, humility is the quiet force that holds people together through life's ever-changing seasons.

This chapter is an invitation to explore how humility can enrich your relationships. It encourages you to embrace vulnerability, practice active listening, and approach challenges with empathy and collaboration. As you delve deeper into this exploration of humility in love, remember that each step taken towards understanding and connection strengthens the bond you share with others.

Transformation Prompt – 5 (Gratitude) and 3 (Habit Tracking)

- Spend time expressing gratitude to each of your family members.

- Consider hosting a gratitude session where everyone can share the reasons they are thankful for each other. Reflect on how humility manifests in these relationships.

- Consider ways in which humility can improve your relationships with your family. Create a habit tracking chart to start implementing specific actions into your daily life at home.

Conflict Resolution:
Humility as a Tool for Peaceful Solutions

Imagine a heated argument where words fly like arrows. Tempers flare, and voices rise, but amidst the chaos, humility acts as a calming force. It's the gentleness that de-escalates tensions, allowing room for understanding to blossom. Humility reminds you to step back and recognize your faults, thereby creating a space where defensiveness dissipates. This self-awareness opens the door to peaceful resolutions, reminding everyone involved that conflicts aren't about winning but finding common ground together.

Humility's power lies in its ability to shift focus from blame to compassion. It's about setting aside pride and asking yourself, "What can I learn here?" Seeking common ground with patience means listening more than speaking, responding rather than reacting. It transforms disputes into opportunities for growth and collaboration. The humble person doesn't shy away from responsibility; they embrace it. By admitting mistakes promptly and sincerely, they pave the way for reconciliation, showing that strength lies in vulnerability and setting the stage for healing.

Applying humility during conflicts requires practical strategies that emphasize openness and dialogue. Constructive dialogue techniques can be game-changers. For instance, use "I" statements to express feelings without pointing fingers: "I felt hurt when…." instead of "You always…." This subtle shift fosters understanding and reduces defensiveness.

Empathy is another essential aspect of resolving conflicts with humility. It's about genuinely trying to see the world through someone else's eyes. Practicing empathy during disagreements means putting yourself in the other person's shoes, considering their emotions and experiences. Listen not to craft your rebuttal but to fully understand their perspective. This approach fosters compassion and opens pathways to resolution, transforming adversaries into collaborators.

Real-world examples highlight humility's role in defusing conflicts. Consider community meetings where tensions run high over local issues. Mediated discussions often utilize humility as a tool for fostering peace. Facilitators encourage participants to share their viewpoints openly while respecting opposing views. These discussions create spaces where mutual respect thrives, leading to solutions that benefit everyone involved.

Relationship counselors also cite humility as a key factor in achieving successful conflict resolution. For instance, in an article from *Focus on the Family*, a counselor describes how couples who "swallow their pride ultimately choose to value their spouse's thoughts, feelings, and needs above their own." This shift in perspective, prioritizing the relationship over the need to be right, can be a turning point during disagreements. By focusing on understanding rather than winning, couples create space for genuine connection and healing.

In community settings, humility fosters dialogue that bridges divides. It encourages individuals to set aside their egos and focus on shared goals. Imagine a neighborhood dispute over a new development project. By approaching the issue with humility, residents can work together to find solutions that respect diverse perspectives and collectively address concerns.

Practicing humility in conflict resolution isn't about ignoring problems or brushing them under the rug. It's about confronting them with grace and empathy, recognizing that every disagreement holds potential for growth and understanding. Humility transforms conflicts into opportunities for connection, fostering environments where peace can flourish.

In relationships, whether personal or communal, humility is the thread that weaves through conflicts, binding individuals with empathy and trust. It's the quiet strength that speaks volumes, encouraging us to listen deeply, respond thoughtfully, and build bridges where walls once stood. As you explore humility's role in conflict resolution, consider how these principles might transform your interactions, creating spaces where understanding and peace prevail.

Parenting with Humility: Teaching the Next Generation

Parenting is a journey of growth, not just for children but for parents too. Humility plays a pivotal role in this dynamic, shaping an environment where learning never ceases. Imagine sitting at the kitchen table, acknowledging to your child that you made a mistake. It might be as simple as misjudging a situation or forgetting an important event. Admitting these missteps doesn't undermine your authority; instead, it teaches your children the value of honesty and growth. When they see you learning from your errors, they learn to embrace their own imperfections. This vulnerability fosters a home where everyone's opinions and ideas are valued, including those of the youngest family members.

Encouraging open communication in your family paves the way for trust and respect. It's about creating a space where children feel safe expressing their feelings and thoughts without fear of judgment. Picture a family dinner where everyone shares something about their day, with each voice given equal weight. This practice not only strengthens familial bonds but also instills confidence in children, teaching them that their words matter. Listening with intent and responding with empathy becomes second nature, reflecting humility's influence on family dynamics.

Anecdotes from parents and educators highlight humility's transformative power in parenting. One parent shared how admitting her frustrations during a challenging time brought her closer to her children. They responded with unexpected maturity and empathy, proving that humility fosters resilience and understanding. Educators often note that children raised in humble environments exhibit greater emotional intelligence and social skills. They're more likely to navigate challenges with grace, valuing collaboration over competition.

Research supports these observations, showing how humility positively impacts child development. Studies indicate that children who grow up witnessing humility learn to appreciate diverse perspectives and exhibit greater empathy towards others. For instance, research has found that parental socialization, where parents model empathic behaviors and create an environment that encourages internalizing values related to empathy, significantly influences children's empathy development. An authoritative parenting style, characterized by high responsiveness and appropriate behavioral control, has been associated with higher levels of empathy in children. This foundation prepares them for future interactions, equipping them with the tools needed for successful relationships and fulfilling lives.

Teaching humility to children requires thoughtful strategies that embed the value seamlessly into everyday life. These could be simple chores or group projects where collaboration is key. Storytelling is another powerful tool; narrate tales of humble heroes who achieved greatness through kindness and empathy. These stories inspire children to act with humility in their own lives, reinforcing the importance of putting others before oneself.

But the impact of humble parenting extends beyond individual families into communities. When parents model humility, they contribute to raising a generation that values kindness and cooperation over self-interest. This ripple effect strengthens social bonds and fosters environments where everyone feels valued and respected.

Parenting with humility doesn't mean relinquishing authority; it means exercising it with compassion and understanding. By embracing humility, you teach your children that strength lies not in perfection, but in the willingness to grow and learn. It's about acknowledging that you don't have all the answers but are committed to exploring them together. This shared journey cultivates resilience, trust, and a deep appreciation for life's simple joys.

As you navigate the complexities of parenting, consider how humility might shape your interactions and influence your children's development. Embrace opportunities to model humility through your actions and words, knowing that each step taken towards humility enriches your family life and sets an example for the next generation.

Humility in Friendships: Deepening Mutual Respect and Trust

Friendships, like any meaningful connection, thrive on a foundation of trust and mutual respect. Humility plays a crucial role in strengthening these bonds, allowing friends to appreciate each other's perspectives and experiences more deeply. When you value your friend's viewpoint, you create a space where diverse ideas can flourish.

Being present and attentive during interactions shows that you prioritize your friend's thoughts and feelings. This attentiveness transforms ordinary moments into meaningful exchanges, reinforcing the emotional connection that underpins true friendship.

Expressing gratitude and appreciation for the little things your friend does can significantly impact the relationship. A simple "thank you" or acknowledgment of their support goes a long way in showing that you don't take them for granted.

Avoid making assumptions about their thoughts or feelings, as these often lead to misunderstandings. Instead, approach conversations with curiosity rather than judgment, seeking to understand rather than impose your own viewpoint. This approach fosters an atmosphere where both parties feel heard and valued.

Challenges are inevitable in any friendship, but addressing them with humility can lead to resolution and growth. Navigating misunderstandings requires patience and a willingness to see things from your friend's perspective. Instead of jumping to conclusions or getting defensive, take a step back and consider the situation objectively. If you've wronged your friend, apologizing sincerely demonstrates humility and respect for the relationship. Just as important is the ability to forgive when your friend acknowledges their mistakes. This reciprocity builds resilience within the friendship, enabling it to withstand the test of time.

Real-life examples abound where humility has played a pivotal role in sustaining lifelong friendships. Consider comedians Kate Berlant and Jacqueline Novak, whose enduring friendship has been a cornerstone of their personal and professional lives. Their bond, formed through shared experiences in stand-up comedy and co-hosting the podcast "Poog," thrives on mutual understanding and respect for each other's boundaries. They emphasize the importance of recognizing each other's limits and personal space, which has only strengthened their connection over time. Their dialogue underscores how a supportive friendship, grounded in humility, can be a powerful source of emotional stability and joy.

Friendship experts also emphasize the importance of humility in maintaining strong relationships. Dr. Robert L. Selman, a developmental psychologist, proposed that the ability to coordinate one's own perspective with that of others fosters a deeper understanding of interpersonal and relational management skills. This perspective-taking, a facet of humility, is crucial in developing and sustaining meaningful friendships. Selman's five-stage model of friendship development illustrates how individuals progress from egocentric interactions to more mutual and intimate relationships, highlighting the role of humility and empathy in this evolution. Furthermore, Selman's research underscores that as individuals mature, their capacity for role-taking enhances, enabling them to navigate complex social situations with greater understanding and cooperation.

Additionally, researchers have found that humility is positively correlated with relationship outcomes such as satisfaction and forgiveness. The more humble individuals are, the better the predicted relationship outcomes, indicating that humility not only opens the door to more relationships but also healthier ones.

The presence of humility in friendships is like the invisible thread that binds people together through thick and thin. It encourages you to focus less on yourself, allowing room for empathy and understanding to take root. When you approach friendships with humility, you prioritize the collective well-being over individual desires, creating an environment where everyone feels valued and important. This mindset transforms friendships from mere acquaintanceships into lasting bonds that can weather life's inevitable storms.

In friendships, humility is not about self-effacement but about elevating one another through shared experiences and mutual support. It's about recognizing that everyone has something valuable to contribute, whether it's wisdom gained from personal experience or a simple act of kindness that brightens someone's day. By cultivating humility in your friendships, you create a space where authenticity reigns supreme, allowing both individuals to grow and flourish by bringing out the best in each other.

As you reflect on your own friendships, consider how humility might enhance these connections. Think about ways to express appreciation for your friends' contributions or how you might approach challenges with more patience and understanding. Embrace humility as a guiding principle in your interactions, knowing that it strengthens the bonds you share and enriches your life in countless ways.

Professional Relationships: The Impact of Humility in Networking

Imagine walking into a bustling networking event, where the room is filled with professionals exchanging business cards and sharing stories. In this environment, humility becomes your greatest ally. It's the quiet confidence that allows you to approach others with authenticity, valuing genuine connections over superficial exchanges. When you embrace humility, you listen more than you speak, absorbing the diverse perspectives that flow around you. This open-mindedness not only enriches your perception, but also signals to others that you are approachable and respectful.

Approaching networking with authenticity means being yourself, not pretending to be someone you're not. People appreciate sincerity and are more likely to remember you when you present your true self. Instead of focusing solely on what you can gain, consider what you can offer. Whether it's sharing resources, knowledge, or introductions, offering help without expecting anything in return builds trust and rapport. This generosity creates a network that supports mutual growth and collaboration.

Humility transforms networking from a checkbox task into a meaningful endeavor that enriches both personal and professional life. It encourages you to engage with others genuinely, appreciating their contributions and learning from their experiences. In doing so, you build a network rooted in trust, respect, and mutual support, qualities that elevate your career and open doors to endless possibilities.

Networking is not just about expanding your contact list; it's about nurturing relationships that inspire growth and innovation. By incorporating humility into your networking efforts, you cultivate connections that last far beyond a single event or meeting. These connections become invaluable assets as you navigate your professional journey, providing support, guidance, and opportunities along the way.

Networking success stories often highlight individuals who have prioritized relationship-building over self-promotion. Consider the story of Melinda Johnson, a graduate of Fairleigh Dickinson University's Silberman College of Business. Instead of aggressively distributing her résumé at networking events, Melinda focused on building genuine connections. Through meaningful conversations and expressing sincere interest in others' work, she reconnected with Bob, an alumnus she met at an HR Alumni Meet and Greet event. This relationship proved pivotal when she learned about an HR representative role at Campbell Soup Company that aligned with her skills and experience. Melinda's humble approach and the strong network she cultivated led to her successfully securing the position.

Many leaders attribute their achievements not to their intelligence or charisma, but to their ability to listen and learn from those around them.

Humility opens doors to career growth by building a reputation for integrity and reliability. When colleagues and peers see you as someone who values honesty and keeps commitments, they are more likely to recommend you for opportunities. This trustworthiness lays the foundation for professional relationships that transcend transactional interactions.

Furthermore, humility attracts mentors who are eager to guide those who demonstrate a willingness to learn and grow. These mentors provide invaluable insights and advice that can propel your career forward.

Examples of humility in professional relationships abound, illustrating its transformative impact. Consider the mentorship between Chris O'Neill, a seasoned executive, and David Joosten, co-founder of GrowthLoop. Early in his career at Google, Joosten demonstrated remarkable humility by actively seeking feedback and acting upon it. When O'Neill recommended the book *Founding Sales* by Peter Kazanjy, Joosten not only read it promptly but also returned with twenty insightful questions, showcasing his eagerness to learn and grow. O'Neill emphasized that such engagement, rooted in humility, amplifies the value of mentorship. This dynamic underscores how a humble approach can foster meaningful professional relationships and drive personal development.

In the world of business and beyond, humility serves as a powerful tool for fostering authentic relationships. It's about being open to learning from others, appreciating diverse perspectives, and contributing positively to the communities you're part of. As you continue building your professional network, remember that humility isn't a sign of weakness but a testament to your strength and willingness to grow.

Transformation Prompt – 2 (Journaling) and 5 (Gratitude)

- Take 10–15 minutes to reflect on a time when you approached a professional opportunity or even a casual conversation with humility rather than self-promotion. Ask yourself:

  » What did I learn by listening rather than leading with my accomplishments?

  » How did that interaction shape the relationship or opportunity?

  » How can I approach future interactions with a more humble and relationship-focused mindset?

- List three people who have helped you grow professionally, whether through mentorship, encouragement, or simply offering you a chance. Write a note of appreciation to at least one of them this week, even if you don't send it. The act of acknowledging their role reinforces a spirit of humility and honors the connection you've shared.

Forgiveness and Humility:
Healing and Reconciliation

The journey towards forgiveness is deeply personal, yet universally understood. It's a testament to the human capacity for growth and compassion. Forgiveness can feel like an uphill climb, especially when emotions run high and wounds are fresh. Yet, at its core, forgiveness requires humility. It's the quiet acknowledgment that none of us are flawless, and we all play a part in conflicts. This recognition isn't about self-criticism; it's about understanding and accepting our role, opening the door to genuine healing. When you humble yourself, you begin to see conflicts from a broader perspective, which is a critical step towards forgiveness.

Humility allows you to let go of the ego's need to be right, making space for reconciliation.

Humility also plays a significant role in reconciling relationships. Imagine reaching out to someone you've had a falling out with, not with demands or expectations but with a heart open to understanding and apology. This act of reaching out can be transformative, setting the stage for peace. Sometimes, it's the small, humble gestures that carry the most weight—a sincere apology, a willingness to listen, or simply showing up when it matters most.

The story of Joe and Amy shows just how powerful humility and forgiveness can be, even in the face of heartbreak.

In 1992, Joe Avila made a life-altering mistake. While driving under the influence, he caused a tragic accident that took the life of 17-year-old Amy Wall. Overwhelmed by guilt and sorrow, Joe took full responsibility for his actions, pleading guilty and serving a prison sentence. During his time in prison, he embarked on a journey of personal transformation, seeking God, serving others in hospice care, and committing himself to a path of humility and healing.

Years later, upon his release, Joe felt a deep desire to ask forgiveness from Amy's family. He reached out, not knowing what kind of response he would receive. In time, he met with Amy's brother, Derek, and eventually her father, Rick. In both meetings, Joe expressed profound remorse for his actions, not to clear his conscience, but to acknowledge the pain he had caused.

In a stunning act of grace, Rick Wall forgave him. Even before Joe could speak the words, Rick embraced him and said, "I love you, Joe." It was a moment of unimaginable beauty, one that turned tragedy into a shared testimony of healing, reconciliation, and the quiet power of humility.

Joe's story reminds us that humility doesn't erase the past, but it can redeem it. When we choose to approach one another with sincerity, remorse, and a willingness to change, even broken relationships can be restored. Forgiveness becomes possible. And healing, no matter how unlikely, finds a way.

> **Forgiveness doesn't erase the past, but it reshapes your future by releasing the power that past grievances hold over you.**

The psychological benefits of forgiveness rooted in humility are substantial. Studies highlight how letting go of grudges reduces stress and contributes to emotional growth. When you forgive, you free yourself from the chains of resentment, allowing peace and happiness to flourish. Embracing humility in this process enriches your emotional landscape, fostering resilience and empathy.

Writing forgiveness letters can be a powerful practice. When you sit down to write, you're not just penning words—you're expressing your willingness to move past hurt and bitterness. These letters, even if never sent, help clarify emotions and intentions. They are a testament to your commitment to healing. In these moments of vulnerability, practicing self-compassion becomes vital. It's easy to be harsh on oneself for past actions, but understanding that everyone makes mistakes can be liberating. It's about offering yourself the same grace you extend to others.

When you choose humility, you choose to see beyond your hurt and embrace the possibility of healing. In doing so, you pave the way for emotional liberation and stronger relationships.

In everyday life, humility, when intertwined with forgiveness, transforms relationships and personal well-being. It's about stepping back from conflict with a willingness to see things differently, offering forgiveness not just for others but for yourself. This transformative power of humility in forgiveness encourages you to mend fences and build bridges where there once were walls. Each act of forgiveness nurtures a spirit of community and connection.

Forgiveness is not always easy, but it is profoundly freeing.

I know from personal experience that forgiveness can be fully embraced even without reconciliation. After leaving a long-term abusive relationship, I came to understand that healing didn't require reentering that dynamic. Forgiveness, in this context, wasn't about excusing the harm or reopening the door to further pain; it was about releasing the hold that resentment had on my heart. If you find yourself in a situation where reconnection is not safe or emotionally healthy, know this: Forgiveness is still a powerful and necessary step. It's what frees you to move forward with peace, dignity, and strength. Sometimes, the most courageous act of humility is choosing to forgive without returning.

Forgiveness is more than an act; it's a mindset fostered by humility. By embracing this mindset, you cultivate a life filled with compassion and empathy, where relationships thrive on mutual respect and understanding rather than resentment and anger. This is how humility leads not only to personal peace but also to a more harmonious world.

Transformation Prompt – 1 (Prayer/Meditation) and 4 (Community)

- Find a quiet space to still your heart and mind. Reflect on any relationships in your life that may be fractured or in need of healing. Offer a prayer or spend time in silent meditation, asking for the courage to approach the situation with humility. Invite wisdom, grace, and strength to guide you, especially if the next steps are difficult or vulnerable.

- Share your reflections with a trusted mentor, counselor, spiritual advisor, or close friend, someone who can offer honest feedback and support. Ask them:

  » What patterns do you see in how I handle conflict or forgiveness? How can I take a humble step toward healing this relationship?

  » Will you walk with me as I take that step?

Humility may open the door, but healing often requires a community that walks with us. Don't be afraid to let someone in.

Humility in Community Service: Serving with a Genuine Heart

Community service thrives on humility. It's the unspoken force that drives individuals to serve not for applause, but because they genuinely care. Picture a volunteer at a local food bank, sorting cans and packing bags, not for recognition, but to ensure someone gets a meal tonight. This is humility in action—serving without seeking personal gain. It's about prioritizing the needs of the community over any personal agenda, focusing on making a real difference rather than merely fulfilling a volunteer requirement.

Being humble in community engagement means collaborating with local leaders and stakeholders to identify what truly matters to those you're serving. It's about listening to their needs instead of assuming you know best. Adaptability becomes key when humility leads the way. You might come in with one plan, but community feedback could suggest another approach. Embracing this feedback and adjusting accordingly shows respect and dedication to the cause. It's not about imposing your vision but aligning with theirs, working together toward common goals.

Humility in service fosters stronger community bonds and trust. When people see that you're there to help, not to lead or take credit, they're more likely to welcome you with open arms. Long-term relationships and partnerships blossom from this trust, setting a foundation for ongoing collaboration and support.

Humility encourages collective action and empowerment, inspiring others to join in and contribute their efforts. This shared commitment strengthens the community from within, creating a ripple effect of positive change.

A powerful example of this can be found in the wake of Hurricane Katrina. In one of New Orleans' hardest-hit neighborhoods, a small group of volunteers chose to serve quietly and intentionally, without fanfare or expectation of praise. Led by roofer Daryl Kiesow, these volunteers arrived in Central City not with grand solutions, but with open ears and willing hands. They listened to residents, respected local knowledge, and worked side by side with those most affected by the disaster. This humble, grassroots approach laid the foundation for what would become the United Saints Recovery Project.

Operating out of a local church, the organization brought together volunteers from across the country and the world to rebuild homes, especially for the elderly, disabled, and disadvantaged. But their efforts went beyond construction. The relationships built during this time fostered hope, restored dignity, and revitalized the heart of the neighborhood. Because the volunteers centered humility in their approach, they empowered the community rather than overshadowing it. The United Saints Recovery Project is a testament to what happens when service is grounded in humility: sustainable change, born not from control, but from collaboration.

This story highlights how humility shapes community service into a fulfilling endeavor driven by a genuine desire to help others. When we approach service with humility, we step back from the spotlight, creating room for others to shine and for communities to flourish. Serving with humility isn't about diminishing oneself; it's about altruism in action, fostering environments where everyone's contributions are valued.

Whether you're volunteering at a local shelter or organizing a neighborhood clean-up, remember that humility is your greatest ally. It's what allows you to connect deeply with those you serve and create a lasting impact. As you engage in community service, let humility guide your actions and decisions. It will enrich not only the lives of those you help but also your own experience, revealing new perspectives and possibilities.

Through humble service, we discover that real change comes not from the loudest voice or the grandest gesture, but from genuine acts of kindness performed with compassion and love. When we serve with open hearts and sincere intentions, we build bridges across differences and unite communities in shared purpose. Let humility be your compass as you navigate the world of service, knowing that every act, big or small, significantly contributes to a larger tapestry of hope and healing.

Transformation Prompt – 3 (Habit Tracking) and 6 (Affirmations)

- Humility grows through consistent, intentional action. This week, commit to one small act of service each day that centers on others rather than yourself. Track your efforts using a simple chart or journal entry. Examples might include:

  » Offering help without being asked.

  » Giving someone else credit or recognition.

  » Listening fully without redirecting the conversation to yourself.

- Begin each day with a statement that roots you in humility and purpose. Choose one or write your own:

  » "I serve not to be seen, but to make a difference."

  » "I release the need for praise and embrace the joy of quiet impact."

  » "Each humble act I offer is a seed of change."

The Role of Humility in Diverse Social Settings: Cultivating Belonging

Imagine walking into a room filled with people from all walks of life, each carrying their unique stories and perspectives. In these diverse cultural interactions, humility emerges as a bridge builder, connecting different backgrounds with respect and understanding. When we embrace cultural differences with curiosity, we open ourselves to learning rather than judging. This mindset transforms cultural diversity from a barrier into a rich canvas of shared experiences. Humility encourages us to listen and learn, allowing us to appreciate the beauty in every culture's uniqueness. This openness fosters an environment where everyone feels valued and understood, creating a harmonious blend of voices and ideas.

Practicing humility in multicultural settings involves more than just tolerance; it requires active engagement. Participating in cultural exchange programs offers firsthand experiences that deepen our understanding of other traditions and customs. These exchanges are opportunities to step out of our comfort zones and immerse ourselves in another culture, breaking down preconceived notions. Learning a few phrases in different languages, even simple greetings or expressions of gratitude, shows genuine respect and willingness to connect on a personal level. This small gesture has a big impact, breaking down language barriers and fostering warmth and connection.

Humility plays a significant role in reducing prejudice and dismantling stereotypes. By encouraging open dialogue about cultural experiences, we challenge biases that often stem from ignorance or misunderstanding. When we share stories and listen to others' narratives, we begin to see beyond stereotypes, recognizing the individuality in each person. This process not only enhances our perspectives but also fosters trust and compassion, essential ingredients for breaking down walls of prejudice. Humility invites us to approach these conversations with an open heart, ready to learn and grow from the diverse world around us.

Inclusive environments thrive on humility, celebrating diversity as a strength rather than a challenge. In these spaces, everyone's voice matters, and differences are embraced rather than feared. Social gatherings that prioritize inclusivity create a sense of belonging for all participants. Imagine attending an event where various cultures are represented through music, food, and art. These gatherings are more than just celebrations; they are affirmations of our shared humanity. Humility allows us to appreciate the richness that diversity brings to our lives, fostering connections that transcend cultural boundaries.

As we navigate diverse social settings, humility is our compass, guiding us toward understanding and connection. It's the quiet confidence that allows us to engage with others openly, without fear or prejudice. It's about recognizing that every interaction holds the potential for learning and growth. By approaching cultural differences with humility, we contribute to a more inclusive and harmonious world.

In closing this chapter on humility in relationships, remember that humility is the thread that weaves through every interaction, strengthening bonds and fostering understanding across diverse settings. It's about listening more than speaking, embracing differences with curiosity, and recognizing that every person has something valuable to offer. As you reflect on these principles, consider how they might shape your interactions in diverse social settings, creating spaces where everyone feels seen, heard, and valued.

In the next chapter, we'll explore how humility leads to inner peace—not by silencing the self, but by helping us step out of the spotlight and align ourselves with something greater. As we've seen, humility transforms our relationships, drawing us closer to others through empathy, forgiveness, and service. But the dance doesn't end there. Just as humility fosters harmony between people, it also invites us into a quieter, deeper rhythm within ourselves. When we stop striving to prove our worth, we find space to breathe, to rest, and to move freely. Let's continue the dance inward, where humility becomes not just a way of relating, but a way of being.

There is no respect for others without humility in one's self.

Henri Frederic Amiel

Chapter 5:

Humility and Inner Peace

Before we can talk about humility's role in inner peace, we must talk about the ego—not to villainize it, but to understand it. The ego is not our enemy; it's a vital part of our human experience. It helps us form identity, establish boundaries, pursue goals, and protect ourselves in uncertain situations. It gives us a sense of "I am," which can be both grounding and empowering.

However, left unchecked, the ego can also lead us astray. It clings to control, seeks validation, and resists vulnerability. It fears being unseen, unheard, or unimportant, and in its striving to protect us from those fears, it can prevent us from experiencing true peace. When ego dominates, we often find ourselves caught in cycles of comparison, defensiveness, and performance.

Humility doesn't eliminate the ego. It loosens its grip. It whispers to the ego, "You're not in control." In doing so, humility creates space for stillness, for clarity, for a deeper connection to purpose and peace.

**This chapter is not about erasing the self.
It's about shifting our inner posture from self-
centered striving to self-transcendent being.**

It's about discovering the courage to be radically humble and boldly compassionate. When the ego is guided, not silenced, by humility, we begin to move through life with unshakable confidence, a steadier joy, and a soul at peace.

Guiding Your Ego: Finding Inner Peace

Imagine you're nestled comfortably in a bustling café, the aroma of freshly brewed coffee envelops you as you sip your favorite latte. Two close friends join you, eager to catch up and share recent news. One friend excitedly describes a recent promotion, radiating genuine joy and satisfaction about this new chapter in their career. The other friend quietly shares their own news with a hint of disappointment, as they admit to feeling overshadowed and grappling with feelings of inadequacy and perceived unfairness. This familiar scenario highlights the ongoing internal battle each of us faces with our ego. It thrives and flourishes in the arena of comparison, perpetually fueling a cycle of personal turmoil and unrelenting stress. Ego-driven thoughts act like a magnifying glass on our insecurities, prompting us to question our self-worth and derive our identity from external achievements and accolades, creating an impermeable barrier to genuine self-expression. The ego maneuvers with whispers that cunningly suggest we are only as valuable as our most recent success or as insignificant as our last failure.

In light of this understanding, it becomes incredibly important to delve into techniques and strategies that can effectively minimize the influence of ego in our lives. Practicing detachment from outcomes serves as a foundational starting point. This approach involves putting forth effort without being tethered to the results, thus freeing ourselves from the clutches of ego. It is not a call for apathy; rather, it is an invitation to recognize and embrace effort as a reward in and of itself. Moreover, questioning ego-driven beliefs is another profound strategy. When faced with doubts or insecurities, pause and ask yourself, "Is this belief empowering me, or is it constricting and limiting?" Such reflective questioning can peel back the layers of illusion cast by ego, unveiling the underlying fears that often parade as ego. By gently dismantling these fears, you gradually guide your ego in the direction of humble empowerment..

Letting go of ego leads to a transformative path toward inner calm and peace. As the grip of ego begins to loosen, emotional stability emerges as a natural byproduct. You find yourself stepping off the roller coaster of emotional highs and lows dictated by external validation, creating space for a nurturing and steady sense of self-worth rooted in the essence of being rather than incessantly doing. This profound shift fosters a tranquil inner landscape where the discord of chaos is replaced by a soothing stillness, and genuine peace integrates into the very fabric of your existence.

As you embark on this enlightening journey through the chapter, remember that ego is not to be perceived as an adversary to be eliminated but rather as an intricate aspect of our psyche to be comprehended thoughtfully and integrated harmoniously with humility. By loosening the firm hold of ego, you open yourself to embrace inner calm and invite the blossoming of true self-expression, paving the way for an authentic and fulfilling existence to flourish.

Transformation Prompt – 6 (Affirmations) and 2 (Journaling)

- Consider embracing daily affirmations that emphasize the richness of your intrinsic value. Consistently remind yourself that your worth is not inherently tied to external achievements; rather, it is an integral component of your very being.

- Use your journal to capture instances when ego dictated your actions or reactions, and explore alternative responses that could have been rooted in humility. This practice fosters enhanced self-awareness and empowers you to consciously choose humility as ego's compass.

The Art of Surrender:
Trusting the Process

Imagine standing at the edge of a wide-open field, arms outstretched, embracing the vastness around you. This image captures the essence of surrender, a concept deeply rooted in humility and acceptance. Surrender isn't about giving up or resigning; it's about acknowledging that some things are beyond our control and choosing to be at peace with that reality. Picture surrender as a gentle acceptance of life's unpredictability, allowing you to flow with its currents rather than against them. It's the difference between feeling frustrated by a sudden storm and finding beauty in the rain. Surrender invites you to release the need for control and embrace the present moment, cultivating humility by recognizing your place within the greater whole.

Incorporating surrender into your life can significantly reduce stress. When you accept uncertainty, you free yourself from the exhausting need to predict every outcome. Think about times you've clung tightly to plans, only to find that life had other ideas. By letting go, you create space for peace, allowing yourself to breathe deeply, even amidst chaos.

Consider the story of Lauren Apfel, a mother of four who consciously chose not to let anxiety dictate her parenting. In a culture where parental worry is often worn as a badge of honor, Lauren embraced a different path. She avoided over-monitoring her children and instead trusted in their resilience and her own steady presence. This surrender brought not only a sense of empowerment to her children but also a deep calm to her own life.

Another powerful example comes from Eldiara Doucette, who was diagnosed with a rare form of cancer at just 19. Over the years, she endured multiple recurrences and eventually underwent an amputation. Rather than resisting reality, Eldiara embraced radical acceptance. By surrendering to what she could not control, she found strength, clarity, and peace, even amid ongoing health challenges.

These real-life stories illuminate a profound truth: surrender is not a sign of weakness; it's an invitation to peace. Whether it's trusting your children's path or accepting life-altering adversity, letting go can lead to unexpected strength and serenity.

To practice surrender, start by letting go of your grip on life's steering wheel. Embrace techniques like mindfulness exercises that encourage acceptance. Spend a few moments each day observing your thoughts without judgment, acknowledging them and letting them pass like clouds across the sky. This practice builds resilience against life's uncertainties and helps you find calm amidst chaos.

Another approach involves identifying areas where you can release control. Maybe it's allowing someone else to take charge of a project or accepting that not everything needs immediate resolution.

By embracing these small acts of surrender, you gradually cultivate a mindset rooted in humility and peace.

One powerful example of this mindset in action comes from Matt Dawson, a former corporate investment banker who made the life-altering decision to walk away from a high-achieving career in finance. Despite his success, Matt felt a persistent emptiness—a sense that something deeper was missing. Trusting the process and surrendering to the unknown, he transitioned into the world of extreme endurance sports. That leap of faith ultimately led him to become a six-time world record-holding endurance athlete. Through surrender, Matt not only redefined success for himself but also found purpose and joy in ways he had never imagined. His story is a testament to the life-changing potential that comes when we let go of rigid plans and allow space for something greater to unfold.

When you trust the process, you open yourself to experiences that challenge and inspire you, leading to personal transformation.

In recognizing the power of surrender, you learn that humility and acceptance go hand in hand with inner peace. Embracing life's unpredictability doesn't mean abandoning ambition or goals; it means approaching them with a spirit of openness and adaptability. As you weave surrender into your daily life, you'll find yourself more attuned to the present moment, less burdened by stress, and ready to embrace whatever comes your way with grace and humility.

Transformation Prompt – 7 (Rest) and 3 (Habit Tracking)

- Plan a moment of stillness. It could be a 10-minute break without your phone, a short walk with no agenda, a quiet afternoon without scheduling anything, an hour of solitude to simply breathe and reflect, or a full day of retreat if your schedule allows. Let it be a time of receiving, not striving. Let it remind you that you don't have to do it all, know it all, or fix it all.

- Then choose one to three habits that help you release control and live with greater peace. These might include saying no to something that drains you, delegating a task, ending work at a set time, accepting help from someone else, or doing one thing slowly and mindfully instead of rushing to finish it. Reflect on your observations after a week and decide whether or not to continue with the same habits or choose different ones.

Humility in Prayer, Meditation, and Mindfulness

Imagine sitting quietly, eyes gently closed, as you settle into a comfortable position. Your breath becomes a gentle rhythm, guiding you into a space of stillness. In this sacred quiet, you may choose to offer a prayer, words whispered from the heart, or simply listen. Whether through structured prayer, silent meditation, or breath-based mindfulness, these practices invite you into a posture of humility and receptivity.

When approached with humility, prayer is not about presenting a list of demands, but opening yourself to divine wisdom and grace. It's a moment of surrender—acknowledging your dependence, expressing gratitude, and asking not only for guidance but also for a heart that is willing to be shaped. Prayer cultivates the humility to say, *"I don't have all the answers, but I trust the One who does."*

Meditation and mindfulness, when interwoven with prayer, offer a profound depth that transforms how we engage with our inner world. Humility in these practices means showing up without the pressure to perform. Each session becomes an opportunity to notice, to learn, and to release judgment. It's about being present to your thoughts, emotions, and spiritual longings—not to control them, but to understand and respond with compassion.

In mindfulness, humility invites you to observe your mind's chatter without getting entangled in it. It's the gentle acknowledgment that thoughts will arise and pass, much like clouds drifting across a vast sky. With humility, you're more likely to approach these moments with kindness, seeing them as invitations to understand yourself and, perhaps, to hear the still, small voice of God more clearly.

Breathwork can serve as both a meditative and prayerful act. As you inhale deeply, visualize drawing in humility and peace. With each exhale, release tension and ego-driven thoughts that no longer serve you. This rhythmic surrender becomes a moving prayer, offering up what is heavy and receiving what is healing.

Guided visualizations can also carry a prayerful intention. Picture yourself walking through a serene forest, where each step embodies grace and simplicity. Invite divine presence into that space. Let it become a sanctuary in your imagination where burdens are laid down and peace is received.

To deepen your experience, try a gratitude-focused body scan. As you mentally scan each part of your body, offer a quiet prayer of thanks. This practice honors your body's role in sustaining your life and grounds you in the humility of being both fragile and strong.

Or practice loving-kindness meditation as a form of intercessory prayer. Begin by extending love and grace to yourself, then to others, including those who may be difficult to love. This quiet offering of goodwill transforms your inner world and strengthens your ability to show up in relationships with humility and empathy.

The benefits of these humble practices extend far beyond the moment. They cultivate self-awareness, soften judgment, and bring clarity amid life's complexity. Case studies have shown that individuals who incorporate mindfulness and prayer into daily life often experience greater emotional resilience, spiritual clarity, and an increased capacity for compassion.

Engaging in these practices invites transformation with gentle intentionality. They encourage you to embrace life's uncertainties with an open heart and mind. Humility reminds us that spiritual growth isn't a linear path, but a continuous unfolding—one marked not by perfection, but by presence.

As you explore these practices, remember: Humility isn't about diminishing yourself. It's about *embracing your humanity* with grace, awe, and compassion. Prayer, meditation, and mindfulness all offer sacred ground where you can lay down your ego and receive something far greater in return: peace, perspective, and a deeper connection to yourself, to others, and to the divine.

Transformation Prompt – 1 (Prayer/Meditation) and 5 (Gratitude)

- This week, set aside five to ten minutes each day to ground yourself in humility. You might say a simple prayer like: *"God, open my heart today. Help me to see clearly, love deeply, and walk humbly."* Or you may prefer silent meditation. In meditation, remember to focus on your breath— receive peace and grace with each inhale, and release control, fear, or self-judgment with each exhale. Let this time anchor you in trust and openness rather than striving.

- Take time to notice and express gratitude for the growth you are experiencing.

Balancing Ambition and Humility: Pursuing More for the Sake of Others

Ambition and humility often seem like polar opposites. One drives you to achieve your dreams and reach for the stars, while the other gently reminds you to stay grounded and connected to what's truly important. But they can coexist in a dance that leads not only to success but to deeper fulfillment. It's about setting goals that aren't just self-serving but also positively impact others. Together, ambition and humility create a balanced approach to life where achieving greatness doesn't come at the expense of losing your soul.

Think of ambition as the fuel that propels you forward, while humility acts as the compass, ensuring you stay true to yourself and your values.

Goals can be both ambitious and purposeful. This doesn't mean lowering your standards or aspirations. Instead, it involves crafting goals with a broader purpose in mind. Focus on the impact your achievements can have beyond yourself. For instance, if you're aiming for a promotion, consider how you can leverage your new role to mentor others or contribute positively to your organization's culture. Goals rooted in service and contribution not only fulfill personal ambitions but also foster a sense of purpose that transcends individual success.

Strategies for maintaining this balance involve setting intentions that prioritize service and love over accolades. Start each day by asking yourself how you can serve your family, community, or workplace in a meaningful way. This mindset shifts the focus from personal gain to collective well-being.

Seeking mentorship is another powerful tool in staying grounded. A mentor can provide perspective, helping you navigate challenges without losing sight of humility. They offer wisdom and guidance, reminding you of the importance of staying true to your core values amidst ambition's pull.

A compelling example of this balance is Hamdi Ulukaya, founder and CEO of Chobani. As his company grew, Ulukaya remained committed to his employees' well-being. He implemented progressive policies, such as offering at least 12 weeks of paid parental leave to all workers, including part-time employees, and raising the starting wage to $15 per hour. Ulukaya also focused on community development by establishing job training programs in partnership with local colleges. His approach demonstrates how ambition, when guided by humility, can lead to sustainable success and a positive impact on both employees and the broader community. He saw growth as an opportunity to do more for others, rather than just gaining financial prosperity for himself.

Humility doesn't stifle ambition; it guides it towards meaningful endeavors.

By balancing ambition and humility, you cultivate an environment where success is both attainable and fulfilling. This synergy allows you to pursue dreams with integrity and purpose, ensuring that your achievements resonate beyond personal gain.

As you reflect on your own ambitions and goals, consider how integrating humility into your pursuits might enhance not only your success but also your sense of fulfillment. Remember that ambition and humility aren't mutually exclusive; they're complementary forces that, when harmonized, can lead you to new heights and deeper satisfaction.

In the hustle of modern life, where achievement often takes center stage, it's easy to lose sight of what truly matters. But by embracing both ambition and humility, you create a path that is rich with meaning and purpose. This balance not only propels you toward your goals but also ensures that the journey is as rewarding as the destination.

Overcoming Fear of Judgment: Embracing Your True Self

Imagine waking up each morning free from the nagging worry about what others think. Humility offers a path to this freedom. We are often enslaved not by others' actual opinions, but by the *stories* we tell ourselves about what they *might* be thinking. Our minds construct narratives that hold us hostage—narratives rooted in fear, not fact. But humility quiets that noise. It allows you to accept yourself just as you are, honestly and unapologetically, diminishing the power that others' opinions, real or imagined, hold over you. When you embrace humility, self-acceptance becomes easier because you're no longer chasing an idealized version of yourself or performing for approval. Instead, you stand confidently in your truth, knowing that it's enough. This self-acceptance is a cornerstone in overcoming the fear of judgment and unlocking deeper, more genuine connections with others.

Strategies to embrace your true self often begin with cultivating self-confidence through humility. Affirmations promoting self-love and acceptance can serve as daily reminders that you are worthy and whole. Phrases like "I am enough" and "I am worthy of love" reinforce your intrinsic value, helping to silence the inner critic that thrives on external validation. Journaling exercises can further deepen this practice by inviting you to explore personal values and reflect on what truly matters to you, beyond societal expectations. When you write about moments of authenticity, you reinforce the belief that being yourself is more rewarding than conforming to others' standards.

When we begin to affirm our worth and reflect on our true values, something profound shifts: We give ourselves permission to be seen. And with that, the walls of fear begin to fall. One man's story captures this beautifully.

Michael, the author of *The Blossoming Self*, spent much of his early life grappling with deep-seated feelings of unworthiness. Conditioned to seek approval from others, he often suppressed his true self to fit into the molds others expected of him. This relentless pursuit of external validation led him into emotionally abusive relationships and a profound sense of isolation. Despite being surrounded by people, Michael felt unseen and disconnected, believing that revealing his authentic self would lead to rejection.

The turning point came when Michael began to confront his internalized shame and self-rejection. He realized that his coping mechanisms, including self-destructive behaviors, were manifestations of his suppressed identity. Embracing vulnerability, he started sharing his experiences through public speaking, despite initial fears and nervousness. In one of his early talks, his anxiety was so palpable that an audience member approached him mid-speech to offer a comforting hug.

Through these acts of courage, Michael discovered that authenticity fostered genuine connections. By shedding the facade he had meticulously maintained, he not only found inner peace but also inspired others to embrace their true selves. His journey underscores the profound impact of self-acceptance and the liberation that comes from releasing the fear of judgment.

And the benefits of authenticity ripple into our psychological well-being. Research consistently shows that people who live in alignment with their true selves experience lower levels of stress and anxiety. One study published in *Mindfulness* (2024) found that self-compassion and authenticity can actually regulate the body's stress response, calming the nervous system and reducing the psychological burden of pretense. Similarly, higher self-compassion has been linked to greater emotional resilience, lower levels of depression, and an overall increase in life satisfaction. When you stop performing for others and start living in alignment with your values, you give yourself permission to breathe and to *be*.

When you live truthfully, stress levels tend to decrease because you're no longer expending energy trying to be someone else.

Self-esteem rises as you begin to acknowledge and genuinely appreciate your unique qualities, not in comparison to others, but as a reflection of your own inherent worth. When you recognize that your value isn't contingent on meeting external standards or gaining approval, you start to build an inner foundation rooted in truth. This quiet confidence fosters a more profound sense of inner peace, as you are no longer at war with yourself or pretending to be someone you're not.

The relief that comes from shedding the weight of pretense is both liberating and transformative. Pretending requires constant vigilance—editing your words, managing perceptions, and anticipating reactions. It's exhausting. But when you let go of that burden, you create space within yourself for authentic joy to rise. Contentment flows not from perfection, but from living in alignment with who you truly are. In that space, life feels lighter, more spacious, and far more fulfilling.

The journey to authenticity doesn't mean you'll never feel judged again. It equips you with the resilience to handle it with grace.

When you're anchored in humility, external judgments lose their sting because you've cultivated a strong internal foundation. This mindset shift allows you to move through life with confidence and purpose, unfettered by the shifting opinions of others.

So, how do you start this journey toward embracing your true self?

Begin by reflecting on what makes you uniquely you. What values and passions define your essence? Let these guide your actions and decisions, rather than external pressures or expectations. Surround yourself with people who celebrate your authenticity and challenge you to grow without changing who you are at your core.

As you nurture self-acceptance through humility, you'll notice an unfolding of freedom and peace within. This process might not happen overnight, but each step forward is a victory in itself. Embrace the journey of discovering who you are beneath the layers of expectation and judgment, knowing that authenticity is the greatest gift you can offer yourself and the world around you.

Reflect on moments when you've felt truly yourself, unburdened by others' views and how that felt. Let these experiences inspire your path forward, reminding you that living authentically is not just a choice but a powerful act of courage. As you embrace this path, you'll find that humility naturally grows, allowing your true self to flourish in all its brilliant imperfection.

Transformation Prompt – 2 (Journaling) and 6 (Affirmations)

- Reflect on a time when you held back part of yourself out of fear of being misunderstood or judged. What were you afraid would happen if you were fully honest or expressive? Now, contrast that with a moment when you *did* show up authentically. What was the outcome? What did you learn about yourself?

- Choose one or two affirmations to speak over yourself each morning this week. Let them root you in truth and silence the need for external approval. Repeat them aloud, write them in your journal, or post them where you'll see them often. Try:

  » *"I am free to be myself."*

  » *"My authenticity invites deeper connection."*

Humility and Vulnerability:
Embracing Imperfection

In a world that often celebrates perfection, embracing vulnerability can feel counterintuitive. Yet vulnerability is essential to developing true humility. It takes courage to admit we don't have all the answers, and there is profound strength in acknowledging our imperfections. Vulnerability opens the door to authentic connection, inviting others to see us as we truly are. When we share our struggles, we create space for empathy and understanding, allowing relationships to deepen and flourish. These shared experiences become the foundation for trust and meaningful connection.

Embracing imperfection is not a weakness; it is a gateway to personal growth. Leaders like Brené Brown have transformed how we view vulnerability by openly discussing their own insecurities and doubts. Her willingness to share personal stories of failure and fear has redefined leadership, revealing vulnerability as a catalyst for strength and change.

In her Netflix special *The Call to Courage*, Brené Brown recounts a powerful moment that illustrates this truth. While swimming with her husband during a family vacation, she expressed feeling deeply connected to him. But his subdued response made her feel rejected. Instead of withdrawing, she leaned into vulnerability and said, "The story I'm making up is that you don't find me attractive." That honest admission opened a deeper conversation. Her husband revealed he was having a panic attack, triggered by a disturbing dream about their children's safety. What could have become a silent misunderstanding turned into a moment of deeper connection and compassion.

Brown's experience shows how embracing imperfection and speaking honestly can draw people closer. As she writes in *The Gifts of Imperfection*:

**Authenticity is the daily practice of
letting go of who we think we're supposed to be and
embracing who we are.**

This quote captures the essence of wholehearted living. When we stop performing and start showing up as our true selves, we create space for healing, connection, and growth. Sharing stories of struggle with humility doesn't mean oversharing; it means choosing moments that resonate and invite real connection. Whether you're reflecting on a difficult project or navigating a personal setback, open-hearted honesty invites others to do the same.

Still, a common misconception lingers: the belief that admitting mistakes will cause us to lose credibility. In truth, owning our imperfections builds trust. It shows integrity, self-awareness, and the courage to grow. Rather than diminishing others' respect, this kind of honesty often increases it. People connect more with leaders and peers who are real—those who admit when they're wrong and are willing to learn. Vulnerability doesn't weaken credibility; it strengthens it by showing we're grounded in truth, not ego.

So how do we practice this in daily life? A powerful starting point is practicing self-compassion. When you extend kindness to yourself in moments of doubt or failure, you create a safer internal space for vulnerability to emerge. Simple exercises like writing letters of self-acceptance can help. Reflect on where you've been, what you've overcome, and how you've grown. Celebrate your journey, not because it's perfect, but because it's uniquely yours and filled with purpose. In doing so, you embody the humility and courage that make authentic living not only possible, but transformative.

The benefits of embracing vulnerability go far beyond relationships. By acknowledging imperfections, you free yourself from the pressure to be perfect. This opens the door for growth and discovery. Setbacks are no longer failures but opportunities to learn and adapt. This mindset shift fosters peace and acceptance, encouraging you to navigate life's challenges with grace.

Embracing vulnerability requires courage, but the rewards are immense. It allows you to connect deeply with others and cultivate inner strength. As you explore your own vulnerabilities, remember that every step toward authenticity is a step toward greater freedom and fulfillment. The journey may not always be easy, but it's one of the most meaningful paths you can take.

In these moments of vulnerability, humility becomes your ally. By accepting imperfection and embracing your true self, you unlock the potential for transformation in your life and relationships. Humility and vulnerability create a foundation for a life filled with meaning, connection, and genuine joy.

Transformation Prompt – 1 (Prayer/Meditation) and 2 (Journaling)

- Set aside a few minutes to sit in quiet solitude—no agenda, no striving. Simply be. In this space of stillness, offer a silent prayer:

  "God, help me release the need to be perfect. Let me rest in the truth that I am already enough."

  Breathe deeply. Let the silence remind you that you are loved without performance, valued without perfection.

- Find a small pocket of your day, just five to ten minutes, to step away from noise, distraction, and expectation. Whether it's a walk, a moment of silence, or simply sitting with a cup of tea, treat it as sacred time. Let your soul exhale. Let stillness restore what striving has worn thin.

Humility and Resilience: Bouncing Back from Setbacks

Think about the last time something didn't go as planned in your life. Maybe it was a project that didn't meet expectations or a personal goal that felt elusive. These moments, though challenging, offer profound lessons if viewed through the lens of humility. Through humility, we learn that setbacks are not the end of the road, but stepping stones on a path of growth.

By acknowledging our limitations, we open ourselves to adapting, which is the heart of resilience. Resilience isn't about never failing; it's about how we pick ourselves up and try again with newfound insights.

In times of setback, humility shifts your perspective from one of self-blame to self-reflection. Instead of fixating on what went wrong, it encourages you to ask, "What can I learn from this?" This mindset transforms challenges into opportunities for growth, fostering a sense of resilience that empowers you to move forward with greater wisdom and strength.

Developing resilience through humility involves practical strategies that can be integrated into daily life. Start with reflection exercises that encourage you to revisit past setbacks with a curious and compassionate eye. What insights can you glean from these experiences? How have they shaped your current approach to challenges? By reflecting on these questions, you build a foundation of self-awareness that supports resilience. Cultivating a growth mindset further enhances this process. Embrace challenges as opportunities to grow and develop rather than threats to your self-worth.

The benefits of resilience rooted in humility extend far beyond individual growth; they ripple outward, influencing personal and professional success. Humility fosters adaptability, allowing you to pivot in response to changing circumstances.

Consider the story of Bethany Hamilton, a professional surfer who, at 13, lost her left arm in a shark attack. Remarkably, she returned to surfing just 26 days later, adapting her technique and equipment to accommodate her new reality. Hamilton's unwavering determination and humble acknowl-edgment of her challenges have inspired millions, illustrating how resilience and humility can transform adversity into a platform for growth and influ-ence. Her journey underscores that setbacks, when met with grace and per-severance, can lead to profound personal development and broader impact.

As Hamilton poignantly expressed in the film *Soul Surfer*: "Surfing isn't the most important thing in life. Love is. I've had the chance to embrace more people with one arm than I ever could with two." This quote encapsulates how embracing setbacks can lead to deeper connections and a more pro-found impact on others.

Other stories of resilience and humility from diverse backgrounds further highlight the universal nature of these qualities. Across cultures and con-texts, individuals have demonstrated remarkable strength by embracing humility in the face of adversity. One such example is Jeshurun Vincent, a Malaysian musician who, at 19, lost his hearing in one ear due to a sudden illness. Despite this challenge, he embarked on a global journey, visiting 102 countries over 69 months, sharing his music and message of hope. What could have been a tragedy, if allowed, has been transformed into an inspira-tion for millions of people.

In your own life, consider how humility can enhance your ability to bounce back from setbacks. By integrating humility into your approach to adversity, you cultivate a mindset that not only survives but thrives in the face of life's inevitable ups and downs. Embrace the lessons that challenges offer and use them as stepping stones toward greater resilience.

This approach doesn't mean you'll never feel discouraged or frustrated, but it equips you with the tools to navigate these emotions constructively. As you continue on this path, remember that setbacks are not roadblocks, but opportunities for growth. Let these stories and strategies inspire you to em-brace humility as a cornerstone of resilience. By doing so, you'll find that setbacks become less daunting and more like invitations to explore new paths and perspectives. As you cultivate this mindset, you'll discover that resilience is not just about bouncing back—it's about moving forward with purpose and strength.

Transformation Prompt – 5 (Gratitude) and 4 (Community)

- Think of a setback in your life that once felt like a defeat. Now, identify three things you're grateful for that emerged *because* of that experience—growth, insight, relationships, or strength you didn't know you had.

- Choose a trusted person—a coach, therapist, mentor, small group, or friend—and share a reflection about a time when humility helped you bounce back from adversity. Talk about how that experience changed you. What did you learn? What would you do differently next time? Let this conversation be a space for connection, encouragement, and renewed clarity.

Living with Intention: Humility as a Daily Practice

Each day is a canvas on which we can paint our lives with intention, guided by humility. Embracing humility as a daily practice involves making choices that align with your core values and aspirations, allowing these choices to shape your path. It's not about rigidly following a plan, but about remaining true to what matters most. It involves pausing to ask, *"Does this decision reflect my values?"* or *"How can I serve others today?"* This intentional mindset fosters personal growth by encouraging deliberate action rooted in purpose and meaning.

Incorporating humility into daily life starts with routine practices. Begin by setting goals centered on your values rather than external validation. Identify what truly matters to you and let these priorities guide your actions, whether it's dedicating time each day to community service or nurturing relationships with loved ones. Daily reflections on intentional living can further enhance this practice. Spend a few minutes each evening contemplating how your choices align with your values. Ask yourself: Did I act with kindness and empathy? Did I prioritize meaningful connections? This reflection reinforces intentionality, helping you remain mindful of your core principles.

The impact of intentional living on overall well-being is profound. People who embrace this practice often report feeling more connected to themselves and others. Their lives are rich with purpose, and they experience a sense of fulfillment that transcends momentary successes.

A lifestyle grounded in humility also fosters a sense of purpose and connection that enriches every aspect of life. By living with intention, you cultivate an awareness of the interconnectedness between actions and outcomes, paving the way for meaningful change. Consider lifestyle changes that promote humility, such as simplifying your commitments to focus on what truly matters or engaging in volunteering efforts that contribute positively to your community. These conscious adjustments create a ripple effect, influencing your surroundings and inspiring others to embrace humility as well.

One striking example is the journey of Michael Sheldrick, co-founder and Chief Policy Officer at Global Citizen. Rather than stepping away from his work to seek personal fulfillment, Sheldrick leaned into his role with deeper humility and greater purpose. Through collaborative leadership and a willingness to listen first, he helped build a movement that mobilized millions to fight extreme poverty and promote global health. His efforts contributed to Australia pledging $50 million toward polio eradication and inspired actions from world leaders. His story demonstrates how humility, when paired with intentional living, can drive both personal growth and global impact from within the roles they already occupy.

As we close this chapter, remember that humility isn't just a virtue to admire. It's a practice to be lived daily. When you live with intention and humility, you create a life rich with purpose, connection, and fulfillment.

In the next chapter, we'll explore how humility can transform entire communities, creating spaces where everyone thrives together.

Continue this exploration by embracing humility as a guiding force in your daily life, knowing that each intentional choice contributes to a more compassionate world.

Knowledge is power. Information is power. The secreting or hoarding of knowledge or information may be an act of tyranny camouflaged as humility.

Robin Morgan

Chapter 6:

The Transformative Power of Humility

You've done meaningful work to get here—reflecting deeply, examining old patterns, and taking courageous steps toward growth. But in this chapter, the dance shifts. This is an invitation to pause and simply *be*. To let the idea of humility settle into your soul more quietly. Instead of focusing on doing more, this chapter invites you to notice more. To breathe. To listen. You'll still find gentle reflections woven throughout, but without the pressure to perform or produce. Think of this as an oasis in your journey—a space to receive, to imagine, and to dream about the kind of leader, neighbor, and human you are becoming.

Dream with me.

Imagine a room buzzing with tension—shoulders tight, eyes darting, hushed conversations swirling just beneath the surface. A company is in crisis. Department heads clutch notes, awaiting instructions. The air is heavy with uncertainty.

Then the door opens, and in walks the CEO. Not in a tailored power suit, but in a navy crew-neck sweater and dark slacks, sleeves slightly pushed up. His salt-and-pepper hair is neatly combed back, yet there's nothing overly polished about him. No entourage. No ego.

He doesn't stride in with chest puffed or voice raised. Instead, he walks with calm purpose, making eye contact as he passes. When he speaks, his voice is steady and warm, deep, with just enough gravel to reveal that he's carried some weight lately. There's no false confidence in his tone, only honesty and care.

He stands at the front of the room, not behind a podium, but beside a whiteboard with nothing written on it yet. "I know this is difficult," he begins, pausing to let the room breathe. "And I want to talk to you, not around you or at you. Just with you."

There's a shift. Heads turn. Eyes lift. Shoulders ease.

He outlines the challenges clearly—no spin, no blame. His body language is open, his hands occasionally emphasizing key points, but mostly resting calmly at his sides. And then, just as importantly, he stops talking. He listens. Really listens. As questions rise, he doesn't deflect or defend; he absorbs, acknowledges, and reflects back the insights with genuine gratitude.

Rather than offering rigid solutions, he invites dialogue. "What ideas do you have? What are we not seeing yet?" he asks, his voice low and sincere.

In that moment, the room no longer feels like a battlefield. It feels like a team. A community. A culture built not on fear, but trust.

This is leadership redefined.

This is humility in action—transforming uncertainty into unity, adversity into alignment. Not by asserting control, but by inviting collaboration. Not by speaking the loudest, but by hearing the most.

> **Humble leadership isn't reserved for CEOs or political figures—it's a mindset accessible to anyone willing to embrace it.**

You don't need a title to lead with humility; just the courage to show up with authenticity, empathy, and a willingness to listen.

This chapter invites you to envision a world where humility shapes leadership. A world where empathy fosters understanding and collaboration fuels innovation. As you explore these stories and insights, reflect on how you can harness the transformative power of humility within your own sphere of influence.

What sets humble leaders apart?

Empathy and active listening. Empathy allows leaders to connect on a human level, bridging divides and fostering genuine relationships. Active listening ensures they truly understand varied perspectives before making decisions. These leaders don't just hear; they absorb and reflect, creating environments where collaboration thrives. They recognize that every individual brings unique insights to the table, and by honoring these contributions, they unlock potential that often goes untapped.

The societal impact of humble leaders reaches far beyond their teams. Their leadership style often results in broader societal benefits: community initiatives, inclusive policies and sustainable development. These projects often lead to improved infrastructure, enhanced education systems, and better healthcare facilities. By prioritizing collective well-being over personal gain, they drive progress that uplifts entire communities.

Aspiring leaders seeking to emulate such figures can benefit from mentorship programs that focus on humility. These programs pair experienced leaders with those eager to learn the art of humble leadership. Through guidance and shared experiences, mentors impart the importance of empathy, transparency, and collaboration. They teach that true leadership isn't about position or power—it's about influence and impact. Through these relationships, aspiring leaders learn that embracing humility can inspire change that resonates far beyond their immediate reach.

If you're seeking a mentor or coach who aligns with your values, start by identifying leaders within your workplace, community, or professional networks whose leadership reflects humility, active listening, and collaboration. Ask thoughtful questions: *Do they lead with empathy? Are they open to feedback? Do they credit their team's contributions?*

You can also explore formal mentorship or coaching programs that explicitly emphasize values-based leadership. Look into organizations like Humble Associates, RBLP, or local fellowships that support leadership development with a focus on character and impact. When reaching out, be clear about your goal. You're not just seeking career growth, you're seeking to become the kind of leader who uplifts others.

Remember, the best mentors aren't always the loudest in the room. They're the ones who see your potential and guide you with care, wisdom, and humility.

In your journey to become a humble leader, remember the profound impact your actions can have. Whether you're leading a team at work or organizing a community event, your approach sets the tone for those around you. By prioritizing humility, you contribute to a culture of openness and respect that encourages others to engage and collaborate meaningfully.

Incorporating humble principles into your leadership style doesn't require drastic changes; often, it's the small shifts in perspective—pausing before reacting, asking more than answering, listening without judgment—that lead to significant outcomes. Over time, these practices become second nature, guiding you toward more effective and compassionate leadership.

This chapter emphasizes that humble leaders are not mythical figures; they are individuals committed to making a difference through empathy and understanding. By following their example and embracing humility in your own life, you have the power to affect meaningful change in your community and beyond.

Take a moment to reflect on a leader you admire for their humility. What qualities do they embody? How do they make others feel seen, heard, and valued? Write down three ways you can bring those qualities into your own leadership. Then take it a step further: reach out to that leader. Let them know what you admire about their approach, and express your desire to learn from their experience. Ask them if they'd be open to sharing their story or guidance. You may be surprised how much wisdom and encouragement they're willing to offer. And in that exchange, you'll take one more step toward becoming the kind of leader the world needs.

Loving People Well: Humility in Everyday Life

In the rhythm of daily life, it's easy to overlook the quiet, steady acts of love that leave the deepest impact. Picture a teacher who stays after school to help a struggling student, not for praise or compensation, but because they genuinely care. They believe in each child's potential and offer their time freely, creating a space where students feel seen, supported, and encouraged to grow. Their humility shines not through grand gestures, but in quiet consistency and selfless care.

Then there's the neighbor who brings the community closer together. Whether organizing clean-ups or checking in on elderly residents, they show up with genuine concern and a joyful willingness to help. They don't seek attention; they simply find fulfillment in contributing to the well-being of others. Their humility becomes the thread that weaves people together, building stronger bonds and a deeper sense of belonging.

Acts like these may seem ordinary, but they're deeply powerful. Think of the bus driver who greets every rider with a kind word and a warm smile. Though it's not part of their job description, they understand the value of human connection. Their small gesture can brighten someone's morning and set a different tone for the day ahead. Humility flourishes in these moments, in the way we treat each other when no one's watching.

And the impact of these individuals reaches far beyond the moment. Their actions often inspire others to do the same, creating a ripple effect of compassion, empathy, and connection. Witnessing humility in action invites us to consider how we, too, can show up with love and presence in our own lives.

Humility isn't about recognition—it's about relationships. You don't need a title or platform to make a difference. You only need a willingness to act with kindness, patience, and genuine care. The ripple effect of this kind of love doesn't just change lives—it reshapes communities into places where people feel safe, valued, and deeply connected.

In a fast-paced world, these moments can go unnoticed. But they are the very moments that shape the fabric of society. When we recognize and honor them, we remind ourselves that real transformation begins in the ordinary—with a kind gesture, a listening ear, a choice to put someone else first.

Take a moment to think about someone in your life who embodies this way of living. Maybe it's a coworker who always lends support without fanfare, or a friend who shows up when it matters most. How have their humble, consistent actions influenced you or those around them?

These stories are not about heroism. They are about humanity. They show us that when we choose humility, we learn to truly see and serve one another. In doing so, we participate in a movement far more powerful than personal success—we help create a world where love leads.

The Ripple Effect:
How Humility Impacts Society

Humility is a quiet force that can transform communities in profound ways. Imagine a neighborhood coming together to build a community garden. It's not about individual recognition but collective joy in creating together and watching something grow. People of all ages and backgrounds dig in, plant seeds, and nurture them together. The garden becomes more than a space—it becomes a symbol of unity, cooperation, and shared purpose. Humble actions like these can lead to broader societal change.

Cultural shifts often begin with small, humble actions. When individuals lead with humility, they redefine what's considered normal or acceptable in a society. In a city struggling with high crime rates, for example, a group of residents might decide to initiate evening patrols—not as vigilantes but as concerned citizens looking out for one another. This simple act of community care can ease tensions, build trust and foster a sense of safety. Over time, such initiatives can lead to significant cultural changes, with communities embracing collaboration over conflict.

Humility also shapes how we relate to one another. In workplaces, schools, and public spaces, humility diffuses conflicts before they escalate. Picture a crowded urban environment where people from diverse backgrounds cross paths daily. When individuals approach these interactions with humility, they listen more and judge less. That shift in attitude encourages understanding and empathy, breaking down barriers that might otherwise lead to misunderstandings or disputes.

One powerful example comes from Clement Sprout, who moved with his family to upstate New York, yearning for the close-knit community he remembered from his childhood in South Africa. Upon settling into their new neighborhood, Clement and his wife, Sarah, decided to host a simple gathering in their front yard to meet their neighbors. Initially uncertain if anyone would attend, they were heartened when several families showed up, leading to meaningful connections. This humble initiative blossomed into a more cohesive and supportive neighborhood, with residents looking out for one another and organizing communal activities. The Sprouts' story illustrates how approaching others with humility and a willingness to connect can transform social dynamics, fostering empathy and understanding within a community.

On a global scale, humility is essential for cooperation between nations. International collaborations succeed when countries set aside pride and work toward shared goals. Consider global efforts to combat climate change—these initiatives rely on nations recognizing their collective responsibility. By approaching the issue with humility, countries acknowledge their past contributions to the problem while committing to finding solutions together. This kind of humility builds trust, promotes innovation and strengthens alliances that transcend borders.

Fostering societal humility requires intentional effort and practical strategies. Community dialogue sessions provide safe spaces to explore humility in action. These gatherings encourage open conversations about how humility can enhance communal life. Participants share experiences and brainstorm ways to integrate humility into daily interactions. Schools and community centers can offer workshops on empathy, active listening, and conflict resolution—skills that embody humble living.

When people prioritize humility in their interactions, they create environments where everyone feels valued and heard. This cultural shift ripples outwards, influencing broader societal norms and fostering inclusivity and cooperation.

The influence of humility on society is far-reaching, touching lives in ways both big and small. It transforms how we relate to one another, encouraging us to see beyond our differences and recognize our shared humanity. Whether through community projects or global collaborations, humility has the power to create a more compassionate world where everyone can flourish.

In a time of global complexity and division, humble action is more needed than ever. It helps us listen more deeply, collaborate more freely, and act with greater integrity. Humility clears space for progress by softening defensiveness and opening the door to understanding, creativity, and collective progress.

As you consider your role in fostering societal humility, remember that change starts with small choices. By choosing to act with humility in your daily life, you contribute to a ripple effect that extends far beyond your immediate circle. Each humble interaction has the potential to inspire others and create positive change.

Humility isn't a one-time decision, but a consistent, ongoing practice—one that, like a river carving a gorge through solid rock, shapes lives over time. Its strength is not in force, but in persistence. With each humble choice, each moment of restraint or grace, the landscape begins to change. It softens even the hardest places—our circumstances and our hearts.

When you embrace humility as a guiding principle, you join a global movement towards greater understanding and cooperation. You become part of a collective effort to build communities rooted in empathy and respect—communities where everyone has the opportunity to thrive.

Humility isn't just about individual growth; it's about transforming the world around us. And it starts with you.

Calming the Storm Around Us: The Expanding Influence of a Humble Life

In Chapter 5, we explored how humility quiets the storm within—settling our inner dialogue, grounding our identity, and creating space for peace. But humility doesn't stay contained inside us. It radiates outward, becoming a calming presence in the lives we touch.

Humility has a soothing quality, like a gentle balm on an open wound. It softens tension, slows reactive impulses, and makes room for grace. As you begin to live with humility, you let go of the need to control every outcome or prove yourself in every moment. This doesn't mean you become passive or indifferent. It means you learn to move through challenges with steadiness and care.

Humility reminds us that not every storm requires a response. Sometimes, the most powerful thing we can do is step back, breathe, and allow peace to rise in the space we've cleared of ego.

It equips us to respond to the world with compassion and understanding. You begin to approach situations not to dominate or win, but to listen and collaborate. This mindset can transform conflicts into opportunities for connection and growth.

Consider the story of Judy Timmons, a retired professional from Midland, Michigan. After retiring, Judy dedicated herself to fostering peace in her community. She became instrumental in designating Midland as a "City of Peace" through the Nonviolent Peaceforce, an international organization committed to unarmed conflict resolution. Judy and her team organized anti-bullying workshops, peace events, and community gatherings, all aimed at promoting understanding and cooperation among residents. Her humble, service-first approach created a ripple effect, inspiring others to engage in peaceful initiatives and strengthening the community's social fabric.

Judy's story exemplifies how humility can be a catalyst for positive change. By choosing to serve quietly and consistently, she helped transform her community into a more compassionate and cohesive place. Her actions remind us that humility isn't about shrinking ourselves but about elevating others and fostering environments where peace can flourish.

The calming influence of humility extends beyond personal relationships. When individuals act with humility, they contribute to an environment where everyone feels valued and respected. This collective energy fosters a sense of peace that permeates social interactions, reducing tension and promoting understanding.

The journey toward inner peace through humility is deeply personal yet universally accessible. As we explore these principles in our lives, we discover that true contentment arises not from external achievements but from internal alignment rooted in humility. It's about finding harmony within ourselves so that we can contribute positively to the world around us.

In embracing humility as a path to inner peace, we learn to let go of what doesn't serve us, be it pride or fear, and embrace what does: compassion, connection, and calmness amidst life's uncertainties.

From Self-Focus to Self-Transcendence: Expanding Beyond the Self

Humility nudges us gently from a me-centered mindset to a broader view of the world. It lifts our gaze from the mirror to the horizon, where the needs of others come into clearer focus. This shift fosters altruism, turning self-interest into selfless service. When we step back from our own concerns, we begin to see opportunities to contribute meaningfully to the lives of others.

It might be volunteering at a local shelter or simply being there for a friend in need. These acts of care become stepping stones toward a more purposeful life, one that finds fulfillment not in accolades but in service.

Take, for instance, someone who leaves a successful corporate career to work with underprivileged children. Initially driven by personal ambition, they discover a deeper satisfaction in watching kids learn and grow. Their purpose shifts from climbing the corporate ladder to nurturing young minds. This transformation illustrates how humility guides us toward seeking the well-being of others over recognition. In these moments, personal goals become secondary to the joy of witnessing positive change sparked by simple acts of kindness.

Community service beautifully illustrates this principle. A group of friends might decide to clean a local park, not for praise but because they understand its value to their community. As they work side by side, bonds strengthen, and a sense of unity emerges. Such projects highlight humility's role in fostering collaboration and shared responsibility. It helps us see that we are part of something greater than ourselves.

A compelling example comes from India, where Versha Verma, a middle-aged social worker, responded with incredible compassion during the devastating second wave of the COVID-19 pandemic. After losing her best friend to the virus, she faced difficulty in arranging transportation for her friend's body to the cremation ground, as many services were either unavailable or demanded exorbitant fees. This profound loss and the challenges surrounding it moved Versha to take action.

Determined to ensure that no one else would endure such hardship, she rented a van, hired a driver, and began offering free hearse services to transport deceased COVID-19 patients to cremation grounds. Donning personal protective equipment, Versha and her team worked tirelessly, often in scorching heat, to provide dignified last rites for those who had no one else. Her selfless initiative not only addressed a critical need during a crisis but also brought solace to countless grieving families.

Versha's actions exemplify how humility can lead individuals to transcend personal grief and challenges, transforming them into agents of compassion and change. Her story serves as a powerful testament to the impact one person can have when guided by empathy and a commitment to serve others.

If you're seeking to embrace humility and achieve self-transcendence, practical strategies can support your journey. Start by volunteering. Volunteering allows you to step outside your daily routine and immerse yourself in altruistic endeavors. Whether it's joining a local charity or participating in global initiatives, these experiences broaden your perspective and deepen your empathy.

Reflection is another powerful tool. Spend time considering your motivations. Are your actions rooted in self-interest or genuine care for others? Journaling these reflections can uncover areas for growth and inspire actions aligned with humility.

As humility becomes a part of your daily life, you'll notice changes in how you relate to people and the world around you. You'll listen more deeply, respond more compassionately and engage with others from a place of understanding.

This shift beyond the self isn't about losing your identity; it's about enhancing it through connection and service. It's recognizing that every action has the potential to make a difference, however small it may seem. By embracing humility as a guiding principle, you open yourself to new possibilities for growth and fulfillment.

Humility challenges us to look beyond immediate desires and consider broader impacts. It invites us to engage with the world authentically, contributing positively wherever we can. Through this lens, life becomes less about personal triumphs and more about collective achievements—achievements that resonate deeply within our hearts and communities.

As you continue exploring self-transcendence through humility, remember that this journey is deeply personal yet universally relevant.

Think about how you can incorporate these principles into your daily life. Perhaps it's volunteering at a local organization or simply taking time each day to reflect on how you can serve others more meaningfully. Each act of humility contributes to a world where empathy and understanding flourish—a world where everyone feels valued and connected.

By embracing humility as a path to self-transcendence, we become part of something greater—a community united by shared purpose and mutual respect. It's here that true fulfillment lies—not in accolades or achievements but in knowing that our lives have made a difference in ways both seen and unseen.

The Global Impact of Humility: When One Life Touches Many

Humility, a profound and often understated virtue, has permeated global consciousness through the inspiring actions and lives of cultural icons who have seamlessly woven it into the fabric of humanity's shared experience. These individuals remind us of humility's critical role in sparking progressive movements and societal advancements. They challenge us to consider how we too can contribute positively to the global tapestry.

One of the most powerful examples of the transformative power of humility on a global scale is the life and legacy of Mother Teresa. A towering figure of selflessness, her gentle yet resolute demeanor illustrates humility in its most resonant form. Mother Teresa did not merely serve the poorest of the poor; she chose to embody their plight, embracing their suffering as her own. Her service in the heart of Calcutta's slums was not solely about feeding the hungry or clothing the naked. It was an earnest endeavor to restore the inherent dignity to those forgotten by society, offering them a glimpse of hope and renewal. Her humility knew no bounds, helping to kindle the flames of volunteerism and charitable efforts worldwide. This quiet mission she undertook underscored a global phenomenon, emphasizing that measurable change often originates from the humblest of beginnings.

What many may not realize is that Mother Teresa extended the same depth of compassion to the wealthy as she did to the destitute. She recognized that material affluence did not shield individuals from suffering, noting that the wealthy often grappled with loneliness, isolation, and poverty of the soul. In a letter to philanthropist Lynne Twist, she emphasized the importance of opening one's heart to the strong and powerful, stating, "You must open your heart to them and become their student and their teacher.... They also are your work." Her humility transcended social and economic boundaries, affirming that every person, regardless of status, deserves love, compassion, and dignity.

The Dalai Lama offers another profound model of humility in action. As a globally respected spiritual leader, he tirelessly navigates the complexities of a fractured world with unwavering compassion and kindness. Despite his stature, he carries himself with simplicity and sincerity, embodying humility's quiet power. His teachings, centered on love, forgiveness and unity, resonate deeply with people across the globe who long for peace. By emphasizing love's ability to heal and unite, the Dalai Lama fosters a worldwide community grounded in empathy. His example offers a blueprint for human connection, one that prioritizes understanding over dominance. Through his speeches, writings, and personal presence, he demonstrates how humility can become the foundation for intercultural dialogue, reconciliation, and cooperation.

On a diplomatic level, humility can act as an invisible bridge over the turbulent waters of international relations. Humble leadership foregrounds peace initiatives through dialogue rather than conflict, guiding nations to prioritize listening and collaboration over pride. When countries embrace humility, they open pathways toward shared understanding and peace. Historical diplomatic breakthroughs often recount stories of leaders choosing the route of humility, prioritizing global harmony over personal or nationalistic prerogatives. This approach illustrates that beyond the immediate gains, humility paves the way for the enduring resolution of conflicts, uniting diverse cultures under a common cause for peace.

Cultural exchange programs further amplify humility's global potential. These exchanges allow individuals to walk in the shoes of others, fostering a deeper appreciation for cultural diversity and universal human values. Such experiences promote enduring mutual respect and understanding, laying the critical groundwork for global cooperation and cohesion. Participating in international conferences specifically dedicated to humility allows insightful dialogue and strategy-sharing. These platforms become crucibles for innovation and collaboration, fostering a confluence of minds all dedicated to the spread and inculcation of humility.

In his 2005 TED Talk, "My Wish: Three Actions for Africa," Bono, the lead singer of U2, passionately addressed the AIDS epidemic and extreme poverty in Africa. He emphasized that these issues are not merely charitable causes but global emergencies requiring immediate action. Bono's humility is evident in his approach; he leverages his celebrity status not for self-promotion but to amplify the voices of the marginalized and to mobilize resources for those in need. He co-founded organizations like DATA (Debt, AIDS, Trade, Africa) and the ONE Campaign to advocate for policy changes and increased aid to combat these crises. His initiatives have contributed to significant progress, such as increasing access to antiretroviral drugs for millions of people in Africa and influencing global leaders to commit substantial funds to fight AIDS, tuberculosis, and malaria. Through these efforts, Bono demonstrates how humility, coupled with action, can lead to substantial global change.

These stories demonstrate that humility is not weakness. It is strength with purpose. It is the power to serve, to unite and to elevate others.

These cross-cultural interactions not only enhance our understanding of humility's role on a global scale, but further magnify its potential to create a connected and compassionate world. By engaging with cultures that place a high value on humility, we gain fresh perspectives, discovering nuanced methods to incorporate this virtue into personal and communal spheres.

As we conclude this chapter, one truth is clear: the impact of humility reverberates far beyond the boundaries of personal development. It carefully lays down the foundation for cultural shifts and societal progress. Through the experiences of extraordinary figures like Mother Teresa and the Dalai Lama, we see how these humble actions initiate transformative changes, reaching into the furthest corners of our global community. As we cast our gaze toward the horizon, embracing humility offers a promising avenue toward greater unity and a shared, enriched purpose.

This chapter's exploration of global humility intricately prepares us for our subsequent discourse on real-world applications to cultivate humility in day-to-day engagements, utilizing the insights gained to facilitate more profound individual connections and significant interactions. As we continue this journey, may we carry forward this spirit of humility with open hearts and clear minds.

We come nearest to the great when we
are great in humility.

Rabindranath Tagore

Chapter 7:
Humility and Resilience

am *thrilled* you've made it here. What a journey this has been—an enthralling dance I've had the privilege of sharing with you. And I know, without a doubt, you have it in you to keep dancing long after the last page is turned. Your impact in this wild, precious world will grow far beyond what you can even imagine. I'm proud of you. I'm thankful for you.

In life's stormy seasons—we all face them at some point—humility becomes an unwavering strength. It keeps us grounded and open to growth when everything else feels uncertain. It cultivates adaptability, allowing us to bend without breaking and to shift without losing our essence. Resilience, when rooted in humility, transforms hardship into wisdom. It doesn't just help us survive adversity—it helps us evolve through it.

In fact, it was one such season in my own life that gave birth to this book.

At age 44, I had just completed my third marathon in Mesa, Arizona, and for the first time, I qualified for the Boston Marathon. But just twenty-five days later, I couldn't walk from my bedroom to the bathroom without assistance. A severely bulging disc was pressing into my S1 and S2 nerve roots, leaving my right leg nearly nonfunctional and in excruciating pain. My plans were completely derailed.

But during seven weeks of medical leave, while resting and recovering, an unexpected door opened—one I had dreamed of for years. One I had quietly been preparing for. And I believe it was only through the lens of humility that I was able to see that painful, disappointing season not just as a disruption, but as an invitation—an invitation to begin.

As Tim Keller once said:

> *"Patience and the ability to not worry and not be really upset when things are going wrong in your life is essentially a kind of humility. You know why? It takes humility to say, well, I thought this is how my life ought to go, but I don't know. How do I know? How do I know what God can see? I can't see the end from the beginning. I can't see from my vantage point my entire life and what's best for me. I don't know."*

Humility helps us navigate life's most difficult moments by reminding us that we are not alone. It draws us closer to God, opening our hearts to receive His grace, comfort, and wisdom. And it connects us more deeply to others, anchoring us in the strength of shared humanity. Like the roots of a tree that hold firm through fierce winds, our connection to something greater than ourselves—both divine and communal—grounds us in times of uncertainty.

When setbacks arise, humility creates space between our identity and our circumstances. It allows us to see failure not as a reflection of who we are, but as part of the path we're walking. This posture fosters resilience by nurturing a growth mindset, one that views challenges not as dead ends but as invitations to grow, learn, and become more.

To build resilience through humility, try engaging in reflective exercises like journaling your thoughts during challenging times. This practice can help you identify patterns and develop strategies for future adversity. Sharing with a counselor, therapist, or coach can also enhance resilience by fostering self-awareness and acceptance. Mindfulness practices like deep breathing or meditation can help maintain humility when faced with stress, allowing you to approach challenges calmly and thoughtfully.

Resilience is not just about bouncing back; it's about bouncing forward with renewed strength and insight.

Two summers ago, I had the opportunity to drive across the Golden Gate Bridge in San Francisco. It was breathtaking—not just for its sweeping views, but for the sheer scale and grace of the structure itself. I was especially captivated by the immensity of the suspension cables, stretching like silver threads through the sky. That moment sparked my curiosity, and I found myself diving into the story behind its creation.

That's the story of Joseph Strauss, the chief engineer behind the Golden Gate Bridge. When Strauss first proposed the idea of spanning the Golden Gate Strait, many experts called it impossible due to the challenging conditions and unprecedented scale. Undeterred, Strauss remained humble, seeking collaboration with other engineers and adapting his designs based on feedback. His perseverance and willingness to learn led to the successful completion of the bridge in 1937, the longest suspension bridge in the world of its time. Strauss's journey exemplifies how humility allows us to separate our identity from our failures, viewing them as stepping stones rather than stumbling blocks. This perspective fosters resilience by nurturing a growth mindset, where challenges are seen as opportunities for development rather than insurmountable hurdles.

Lifelong Learning:
Staying Open to Growth and Change

Every day offers the chance to learn something new, and humility serves as our guide through these endless opportunities for growth. Lifelong learning resembles exploring a vast library, each book a new adventure waiting to be discovered. Embracing humility in this context means acknowledging that no matter how much we know, there's always more to uncover.

Take Dr. Craig Fennie, a materials scientist and professor at Cornell University. Despite his expertise in computational and theoretical materials physics, Fennie remains a humble learner, continually seeking knowledge beyond his immediate field. His approach involves combining the tools of theoretical physics with solid-state chemistry to discover new materials with desirable electrical, magnetic, and optical properties. This interdisciplinary curiosity has led to groundbreaking innovations, such as developing materials with combined electrical and magnetic states, opening possibilities for advancements in digital data storage.

What makes Fennie remarkable isn't just his expertise. It's his humility—the willingness to learn beyond his field, to remain teachable. By acknowledging the limits of his knowledge and embracing a mindset of continuous learning, he made significant contributions to materials science. His story exemplifies how humility keeps the mind agile and the spirit young, enabling us to draw connections across disciplines and transform challenges into opportunities for development.

To cultivate a lifelong learning mindset, begin by seeking out new experiences that challenge your comfort zone. Attend workshops on topics you've never explored before or dive into multidisciplinary studies that broaden your perspective. Make it a goal to try something new every month, whether it's learning a language, picking up an instrument, or engaging in cultural exchanges. These experiences enrich your understanding of the world and nurture your humility by reminding you of the vastness of knowledge yet to be uncovered.

Humility enhances our ability to absorb and apply new knowledge effectively. It makes us receptive to fresh ideas and less constrained by preconceived notions.

Testimonials from lifelong learners highlight how humility fuels their passion for knowledge. They often say, "I realized that every person I meet knows something I don't. That keeps me humble and hungry for learning." This perspective not only deepens relationships but also creates an endless loop of learning and growth.

The connection between humility and learning is profound. It empowers us to remain students in life, regardless of our achievements or accolades. By embracing this mindset, we open ourselves to a world rich with possibilities—a world where every encounter becomes an opportunity for growth and understanding.

As you navigate your own path of lifelong learning, remember that humility is your steadfast companion. Whether you're attending a seminar on quantum physics or chatting with a neighbor about gardening tips, approach each experience with humble curiosity. You never know what unexpected wisdom might enrich your life.

Through humility, we find the courage to step into the unknown with excitement rather than fear. And it's that attitude that transforms ordinary moments into extraordinary opportunities.

So keep learning, keep exploring, and let humility guide you toward new horizons filled with endless possibilities.

Community and Humility: Building a Supportive Network

Life is enriched by friends who aren't afraid of telling you the truth. They become accountability partners, playing a vital role in reinforcing humility. They act as mirrors, reflecting your actions and intentions to help you stay grounded. When you're accountable, you consciously seek feedback, allowing humility to flourish. It's not about being critiqued, but about creating checks and balances that manage pride. These partnerships provide a safety net as you navigate personal and professional growth.

Community also plays a crucial role in building resilience. When you face setbacks or obstacles, your accountability partners provide encouragement and guidance, helping you navigate difficult situations with humility. Their presence reminds you that you're not alone.

A supportive network of trusted individuals can be a game-changer in your journey toward humility. Imagine being surrounded by people who genuinely care about your development. They offer constructive feedback, not to bring you down but to elevate you. Peer feedback becomes a powerful tool for growth, offering insights you might overlook on your own. Support groups focused on humility provide a safe space to share experiences and learn from one another. Within these networks, humility thrives as members encourage each other to stay true to their values.

Building this kind of network requires intentional effort. Start by connecting with like-minded individuals who share your values and aspirations. Attend community events, workshops or join forums focused on personal growth and community building. Engaging with people who are committed to similar paths can provide invaluable support and encouragement. These interactions create a sense of belonging, reinforcing your commitment to living humbly.

In summary, accountability partners and supportive networks play an essential role in maintaining humility throughout life's challenges. They offer valuable feedback and encouragement, fostering an environment where you can thrive personally and professionally while staying true to your values of humility.

Celebrating Wins: Recognizing Progress Without Pride

Every step forward is a victory worth acknowledging. Recognizing progress is crucial, not just for motivation but for reinforcing humility. When you celebrate milestones, however minor, it's like planting a flag that says, "I'm moving forward." A simple acknowledgment of learning a new skill or improving a habit can serve as a gentle reminder of your capability and dedication. Yet, it's essential to celebrate without letting pride take the stage. Humility ensures these celebrations remain grounded, acknowledging the journey without overshadowing the process.

Balancing pride and humility is like walking a tightrope. It's about celebrating victories, expressing gratitude, and valuing where you are on the journey without self-exaltation. Instead of seeing success as a solo endeavor, recognize the support and circumstances that enabled it. Sharing successes with humility involves telling your story with grace, acknowledging those who contributed along the way. This approach not only keeps you grounded but also inspires others by demonstrating that accomplishments are communal efforts.

Celebrating the wins of others is another powerful way to cultivate humility. Noticing and acknowledging others' successes enhances your own humility by shifting focus outward. Creative ways to celebrate others include writing a heartfelt note, organizing gatherings where achievements are honored collectively or simply offering sincere praise. Look at leaders who celebrate team successes by highlighting individual contributions during meetings or company events; these gestures build a culture of appreciation and humility.

Receiving praise with humility is equally important. This is an art form that many find challenging. It's easy to think that humility requires rejecting all forms of praise, but this isn't the case. It's about accepting recognition with grace. Implementing a heart check when you receive praise allows you to accept it graciously without letting it inflate your ego. It allows you to respond thoughtfully, acknowledging the compliment while expressing gratitude for those who contributed to your success. You might say, "Thank you, I couldn't have done it without my team's support." This approach reinforces the interconnected nature of achievements and keeps pride in check.

Celebrating with humility requires awareness and intentionality. It's about recognizing progress without letting pride overshadow the journey. When you celebrate humbly, you reaffirm your commitment to growth and create a positive ripple effect that inspires others. Acknowledging the successes of others deepens your own humility, shifts the focus outward and fosters more meaningful connections.

Humility in Legacy: Leaving a Lasting Impact

Legacy isn't about grand monuments, titles or wealth—it's about the quiet, enduring impact you leave behind. A humble legacy shapes future generations by instilling values that continue to inspire long after you're gone. It isn't measured by accolades but by your contributions to society and the principles you impart.

Consider humble leaders like Mother Teresa and Nelson Mandela. Their legacies were not defined by wealth or power, but by their commitment to compassion, service and integrity. Their humility paved the way for future leaders to emulate their principles, impacting countless lives.

What values do you wish to pass down? Kindness? Compassion? A commitment to service? These are the intangible gifts that shape communities and inspire future generations to live with similar convictions.

Building a humble legacy requires intentionality. Engage in mentorship, guiding others with wisdom and empathy. By investing in people, you're creating a legacy that lives through them. Create initiatives that prioritize community and global benefits—projects that uplift others and address pressing issues. Whether through volunteering, advocacy or everyday kindness, your actions form a blueprint others can follow. As you mentor others, foster an environment where humility is cherished, not as a weakness but as strength in service to others.

Examples of humble legacies abound, from philanthropists who quietly support causes to families who instill humility in their children. One remarkable example is José "Pepe" Mujica, former President of Uruguay. Known for his austere lifestyle, Mujica chose to live in a modest farmhouse on the outskirts of Montevideo rather than the presidential palace. He drove a 1987 Volkswagen Beetle and donated around 90% of his $12,000 monthly salary to charities benefiting the poor and small entrepreneurs. He showed that power, when paired with humility, becomes a great tool for unity.

In creating your own humble legacy, focus on the impact you wish to make rather than the recognition you'll receive. Think about how you can contribute to society in meaningful ways. Remember that a humble legacy is built on the principles you embody each day and the influence you have on others' lives. Ask yourself: "What impact do I want to leave behind? How can I invest in causes that will outlive me?" Your humble contributions may not be celebrated with fanfare, but they'll resonate deeply within the hearts of those who are touched by your kindness and integrity.

Preparing for the Future: Humility in a Changing World

In a world where the only constant is change, humility is your best ally. It keeps you open to new ideas and perspectives. It encourages you to embrace technological advancements without fear but with curiosity, viewing them as opportunities to grow rather than threats to resist.

When you approach the future with humility, you become a lifelong learner. You're more willing to experiment, make mistakes and learn from them. This mindset fosters innovation because you're not tied to being right—you're committed to discovering what works.

To prepare for what lies ahead with humility, actively seek out learning opportunities that focus on tomorrow's challenges. These could be workshops on emerging technologies or courses that explore future societal trends. Engaging in such activities not only expands your knowledge but also reinforces your humble approach to learning.

Participate in community discussions about future challenges, where diverse perspectives converge. These conversations can broaden your understanding and provide insights into how humility can guide you through uncertainty. They also remind you that you're not alone in navigating uncharted waters.

On a global scale, humility is crucial in addressing future challenges. It fosters collaboration among nations, encouraging them to work together rather than compete. Whether it's addressing climate change, poverty, or health equity, humble approaches emphasize empathy and shared responsibility. When countries come together with humility, they can achieve remarkable outcomes that benefit humanity as a whole.

Embracing Humility as a Way of Life:
Final Thoughts

As we reflect on humility as a way of life, I want you to remember that it is a constant state of being rather than a destination. It's not a skill to master but a quality to nurture continuously.

Throughout this journey, we've explored humility's interconnectedness with personal growth and meaningful impact. From navigating challenges with grace to fostering relationships that uplift, humility is the common thread that weaves through every aspect of our lives. It reminds us that growth is a lifelong process. The lessons learned here are not just about becoming a better person but about enhancing the well-being of those around us.

One of humility's beauties lies in its versatility. In the workplace, humility opens doors to collaboration and innovation, allowing us to lead with empathy rather than ego. In our personal lives, it deepens our relationships by encouraging genuine connections based on mutual respect and understanding. And within communities, it fosters unity and compassion, creating environments where everyone feels valued and heard.

Living a humble life brings immense rewards. Perhaps the most significant is inner peace—the powerful confidence that comes from aligning our actions with our values. Humility frees us from the need for constant validation, allowing us to find contentment within ourselves. This peace extends to our relationships, strengthening bonds and building trust through authenticity and empathy. Communities benefit too, as humility encourages collaboration and collective growth. When we live humbly, we're reminded that we are part of something greater than us.

So as you continue on this path, embrace humility holistically. Let it permeate every facet of your life, guiding your decisions and interactions. Surround yourself with people who challenge you, encourage you, and help you stay grounded. Seek out communities that support humble living, where shared values create a sense of belonging and purpose.

In this ever-changing world, humility is a steady companion. It keeps us anchored while encouraging bold, meaningful action. It offers us the chance to connect deeply with others, to learn continuously, and to contribute meaningfully to the world around us. As we embrace humility as a way of life, we become beacons of compassion and understanding, inspiring others to do the same.

As we close this chapter, remember that humility is not a destination but a way of being—one that enriches every aspect of life. Let it guide you as you navigate the complexities of this world with grace and integrity, knowing that your humble actions have the power to create lasting change. Carry these lessons with you, letting them illuminate your path toward greater fulfillment and connection.

Conclusion

s we come to the end of this dance, know that another song is already beginning, one meant just for you, inviting you to carry this momentum into the next chapter of your life.

Throughout these pages, we've explored humility, a powerful yet often misunderstood virtue, and uncovered its true essence. We've learned that humility is not about shrinking or silencing yourself. It's about standing with grounded confidence, recognizing your place in a story far greater than your own. It's the quiet courage to use your strength not for the spotlight, but for service.

Together, we've challenged the myths that paint humility as weakness, and revealed it instead as one of the most profound sources of resilience, connection, and strength.

Along the way, we introduced seven transformative tools designed to weave humility into the fabric of your life:

- Prayer or meditation connects you to a force greater than yourself, grounding you in moments of chaos and calm alike.

- Journaling helps you reflect and gain clarity, allowing you to understand your thoughts and actions better.

- Habit tracking encourages awareness of behaviors, supporting intentional change.

- Community offers a support system that challenges and uplifts you.

- Gratitude shifts your focus to the positives, nurturing a sense of abundance and celebration.

- Affirmations reinforce your strengths and capabilities, building confidence without arrogance.

- Rest reminds you to pause and recharge, fostering resilience.

These tools, when used consistently, bolster personal growth, enrich relationships, enhance leadership, and bring lasting peace.

We also explored common challenges that come with embracing humility. You may find it difficult to balance humility with confidence or struggle to practice humility in a world that often rewards self-promotion. But you are not without support. The strategies we discussed—from role-playing scenarios to mindfulness practices—equip you with the right toolkit you need in your journey.

Take a moment to reflect on your own journey through these pages. How has your understanding of humility evolved? Maybe you've become more aware of the subtle ways humility can transform interactions and decisions. Perhaps you've started to see humility as a guide that leads you toward a more fulfilled life.

Now, I invite you to continue this journey. Integrate humility into your daily life. Use the exercises and strategies regularly to keep humility at the forefront of your actions and decisions. This isn't a one-time practice but an ongoing progression.

Share your experiences and insights with others. Engage with your community. When you talk about humility, you encourage a culture of mutual respect and understanding. You use your stories to inspire others to explore humility and its transformative power.

Thank you for embarking on this journey with me. Your commitment to personal and collective growth is courageous and deeply inspiring. I'm grateful we've had the chance to explore this path together, step by step, page by page.

But the dance doesn't end here.

As this chapter closes, a new rhythm begins. Let the music of humility continue to guide your steps—sometimes slow and reflective, other times bold and joyful. Stay connected to what you've learned. Seek out others who are learning, growing, and moving to the same rhythm. Whether through a community group, a meaningful conversation, a journal entry, or a moment of stillness, keep dancing because this world needs the kind of grace, wisdom, and strength that only you can bring.

May your life be a living legacy of humility—strong, steady, and beautifully impactful.

Go forward with courage. The dance is yours now.

References

10 Influential People Showed The World That Humility Is...
https://www.indiatimes.com/trending/human-interest/world-leaders-humble-habits-simplicity-is-all-that-matters-376449.html

Analia's Story: Rodriguez, A. (2015). Eli's Impact. Siblings with a Mission. Retrieved from
https://www.siblingswithamission.org/elis-impact.html

Apfel, Lauren. "Confessions of a Mom Who Doesn't Worry." Motherwell Magazine, January 5, 2017.

Biography.com Editors. (n.d.). Bill Nye Biography. Biography. Retrieved April 22, 2025, from
https://www.biography.com/personality/bill-nye

Bissme, S. (2020, May 6). The Music of his Heart. The Sun Daily. Retrieved from
https://www.thesundaily.my/style-life/the-music-of-his-heart-CB2377316

Bono. (2005, February). My Wish: Three Actions for Africa [Video]. TED. Retrieved from https://www.ted.com/talks/bono_my_wish_three_actions_for_africa

Brown, B. (2019). The Call to Courage [Netflix Special]. Netflix.

Brown, B. (2010). The Gifts of Imperfection: Let Go of Who You Think You're Supposed to Be and Embrace Who You Are. Hazelden Publishing.

Cornell Engineering. (n.d.). Craig Fennie Revisited. Retrieved from
https://www.engineering.cornell.edu/about/branding-microsite/independent-thinkers/faculty-stories/craig-fennie-revisited

Cultural Humility in International Relationship Research.
https://onlinelibrary.wiley.com/doi/full/10.1111/pere.12563

Davis, Don E., M. Brent Donnellan, and Jason Blommel. "Humility and Emotional Well-Being: Self-Compassion as a Mediator." Journal of Positive Psychology, 7(3), 2012, pp. 247–262.

Davis, Don E., et al. "The Prosocial Contours of Humility: Explicit Self-Concept, Relationship Quality, and Relational Behaviors." Journal of Positive Psychology, 8(5), 2013, pp. 444–454.

Dawson, Matt. "Matt Dawson | Six Time World Record Holding Endurance Athlete." The Fallible Man Podcast, Episode Page, 2023.

Doucette, Eldiara. "My Rare Cancer Has Recurred 3 Times in 3 Years. At Age 22, I've Learned to Radically Accept My Fate." People, January 9, 2025.

Exline, Julie J., and Ann L. Geyer. "Perceptions of Humility: Implications for Self and Other." Journal of Positive Psychology, 1(1), 2004, pp. 18–29.

Ferrari, M., Hunt, C., Harrysunker, A., Abbott, M. J., Beath, A. P., & Einstein, D. A. (2019). Self-compassion interventions and psychosocial outcomes: A meta-analysis of RCTs. Mindfulness, 10(8), 1455–1473. https://doi.org/10.1007/s12671-019-01134-6

Forbes Staff. (2013, May 15). Bono: The rock star as activist. Forbes. Retrieved from
https://www.forbes.com/sites/forbeslife/2013/05/15/bono-the-rock-star-as-activist/

Golden Gate Bridge, Highway and Transportation District. (n.d.). Joseph Strauss – Bridge Construction. Retrieved from
https://www.goldengate.org/bridge/history-research/bridge-construction/joseph-strauss/

Great Leaders Balance Ambition with Humility.
https://hbr.org/podcast/2024/02/great-leaders-balance-ambition-with-humility

Greene, Emily Harris. "Joe and Amy: A Story of Reconciliation." Prison Fellowship, July 20, 2021.
https://www.prisonfellowship.org/2021/07/joe-amy-story-reconciliation/

Hamilton, B. (n.d.). About & Biography. Bethany Hamilton. Retrieved April 20, 2025, from https://bethanyhamilton.com/about-biography

How Humble Leaders Foster Resilience. https://www.psychologytoday.com/us/blog/hope-resilience/201902/how-humble-leaders-foster-resilience

How Humility Can Help New Parents Get Along. https://greatergood.berkeley.edu/article/item/how_humility_can_help_new_parents_get_along

How Humility Strengthens Your Relationship. https://psychcentral.com/blog/how-humility-strengthens-your-relationship

Humble Leaders Achieve Promotion Through Mentoring. https://brancher.com.au/blog/career-growth-how-humble-leaders-can-ascend-organisational-hierarchies-through-mentorship

Humility in Leadership: The Unsung Skill of Great Leaders. https://www.betterup.com/blog/humility-in-leadership

Intellectual Humility – Your Fuel for Lifelong Learning. https://gaborgeorgeburt.com/blog/intellectual-humility/370

Is Self-Promotion On Social Media Savvy Or Arrogant? https://www.forbes.com/sites/danabrownlee/2019/02/27/is-self-promotion-on-social-media-savvy-or-arrogant/

Jacobs, J. (Host). (2021, February 19). Good Things #6: Tales from a hearing-impaired travelling musician [Audio podcast episode]. In Live & Learn. BFM 89.9. Retrieved from https://www.bfm.my/podcast/the-bigger-picture/live-%26learn/good-things-6-tales-from-a-hearing-impaired-travelling-musician

Kilbane, Brennan. "Comedians Kate Berlant and Jacqueline Novak on the Healing Power of Friendship." Allure, 3 Aug. 2021.

Leadership in Action: Patagonia Case Study. https://www.thepeoplespace.com/practice/articles/leadership-action-patagonia-case-study

Leadership Lessons from Satya Nadella. https://jdmeier.com/leadership-lessons-from-satya-nadella/

Leader Humility and Employees' Creative Performance – Frontiers in Psychology. https://www.frontiersin.org/journals/psychology/articles/10.3389/fpsyg.2024.1278755/full

Life Lessons From the World's Poorest President. (2015, February 2). Fair Observer. Retrieved from https://www.fairobserver.com/politics/life-lessons-from-the-worlds-poorest-president-43453/

MacArthur Foundation. (2013, September 25). Craig Fennie. Retrieved from https://www.macfound.org/fellows/class-of-2013/craig-fennie

McNamara, S. (Writer), & McNamara, S. (Director). (2011). Soul Surfer [Film]. Sony Pictures.

Mindfulness-Based Relationship Enhancement Benefits. https://www.verywellmind.com/understanding-mindfulness-based-relationship-enhancement-4685242

Miklikowska, M. (2018). "Empathy and Moral Development in Adolescence: The Mediating Role of Parental Empathy." Frontiers in Psychology, 9, 1256. https://www.ncbi.nlm.nih.gov/pmc/articles/PMC6533135/

Mishra, A. (2021, April 27). Lucknow woman starts free hearse service for Covid victims. India Today. Retrieved from https://www.indiatoday.in/coronavirus-outbreak/story/lucknow-woman-starts-free-hearse-service-for-covi-victims-1795610-2021-04-27

Modesty and Humility – Stanford Encyclopedia of Philosophy. https://plato.stanford.edu/entries/modesty-humility/

Mohan, Pavithra. "Chobani CEO: Why We're Now Giving All Workers at Least 12 Weeks of Parental Leave." Fast Company, March 21, 2025.

Nair, S. (2024, April 29). Former President of Uruguay Admired For His Humble Lifestyle, Dedication to Serving His People. MENAFN. Retrieved from https://menafn.com/1109080520/Former-President-of-Uruguay-admired-for-his-humble-lifestyle-dedication-to-serving-his-people

National Science Foundation. (2014, April 4). First Principles Approach To Creating New Materials. Retrieved from https://www.nsf.gov/news/first-principles-approach-creating-new-materials

NPR Staff. (2016, August 21). 11-Year-Old Entrepreneur Launches Lemonade Business With A Mission To Save Bees. NPR. Retrieved from https://www.npr.org/2016/08/21/490721304/11-year-old-entrepreneur-launches-lemonade-business-with-a-mission-to-save-bees

Nye, B. (2015). Unstoppable: Harnessing Science to Change the World. St. Martin's Press. p. 370.

ONE Campaign. (n.d.). About. Retrieved April 21, 2025, from https://www.one.org/us/about/

O'Neill, Chris. "The Power of Humility in Mentorship." LinkedIn, October 16, 2023. https://www.linkedin.com/posts/croneill_leadership-mentorship-humility-activity-7250192217150021633-Zp2c

Pasciolla, I. (2024, December 23). Citizen of the Year Finalist: Judy Timmons. Midland Daily News. Retrieved from https://www.ourmidland.com/news/article/judy-timmons-advocating-world-peaceful-resolutions-19988226.php

Press Trust of India. (2023, June 11). This UP Woman, 44, Ensures Unclaimed Bodies Get an Honourable Cremation. NDTV. Retrieved from https://www.ndtv.com/india-news/this-up-woman-44-ensures-unclaimed-bodies-get-an-honourable-cremation-4111541

Quinn, Michael. The Blossoming Self: Embracing the Journey of Becoming. Heartroot Publishing, 2022.

Quote by Mother Teresa: "Humility is the mother of all virtues..." https://www.goodreads.com/quotes/559677-humility-is-the-mother-of-all-virtues-purity-charity-and

Quotes.net. (n.d.). Soul Surfer Quotes. Retrieved April 20, 2025, from https://www.quotes.net/mquote/1067269

Random Acts of Humility – Word, Life, Light. https://word-life-light.com/random-acts-of-humility/

Selman, Robert L. "Friendship and Peer Relationships." In Encyclopedia of Adolescence, edited by Roger J.R. Levesque, Springer, 2011.

Servant Leadership: Characteristics, Pros and Cons.
https://www.investopedia.com/terms/s/servant-leadership.asp

Silberman College of Business, FDU. "From PDP to Professional — Melinda
Johnson's BS '21 Networking Success Story." Medium, April 13, 2023.
https://medium.com/@fdusilberman/from-pdp-to-professional-
melinda-johnsons-bs-21-success-story-1f6a26aebf8d

Smalley, G. (2024, May 3). Humility Makes a Difference in Marital Conflict. Focus on the Family.
https://www.focusonthefamily.com/marriage/humili-
ty-makes-a-difference-in-marital-conflict/

Sprout, C. (n.d.). Love Thy Neighbor: He Made His Dream of Community Come True. Guideposts. Retrieved April 21, 2025, from
https://guideposts.org/inspiring-stories/love-thy-neighbor-he-
made-his-dream-of-community-come-true/

Stylianou, N. (2013, December 13). Is Uruguay's president José Mujica
the world's most humble leader? The Guardian. Retrieved from
https://www.theguardian.com/world/2013/dec/13/uruguay-presi-
dent-jose-mujica-humble-leader-donates

Svendsen, J. L., Osnes, B., Binder, P.-E., Dundas, I. (2024). Trait self-compassion and perceived stress: A meta-analysis and review of the
mechanisms. Mindfulness, 15(2), 371–388.
https://doi.org/10.1007/s12671-024-02383-w

The End of Ego: Reclaiming Inner Peace.
https://fxmed.co.nz/the-end-of-ego-reclaiming-inner-peace/

The How of Communication: A Case for Integrity, Humility, and
Curiosity.
https://inallthings.org/the-how-of-communication-a-case-for-in-
tegrity-humility-and-curiosity/

"The Importance of Being Humble." Florida Atlantic University, Thrive
Thursdays.
https://www.fau.edu/thrive/students/thrive-thursdays/humble/
index.php

The Most Successful Companies Have Humble Leaders.
https://www.inc.com/adam-robinson/this-1-leadership-quality-
will-motivate-your-employees-to-do-great-work.html

The Power of Gratitude and Humility in Business – Forbes.
https://www.forbes.com/sites/allbusiness/2024/11/05/the-pow-
er-of-gratitude-and-humility-in-business/

The Role of Humility in Building Lasting Peace.
https://mooreliberationtheology.com/role-humility-build-
ing-lasting-peace/

The Wisdom of Humility in Yoga Practice.
https://yogauonline.com/yoga-practice-teaching-tips/yoga-teach-
ing/the-wisdom-of-humility-in-yoga-practice/

Tremlett, G. (2014, September 18). José Mujica: Is This The World's Most
Radical President? The Guardian. Retrieved from
https://www.theguardian.com/world/2014/sep/18/-sp-is-this-
worlds-most-radical-president-uruguay-jose-mujica

Tripathi, N. (2021, May 20). This Social Worker From Lucknow Cremates
Covid-19 Victims for Free. Forbes India. Retrieved from
https://www.forbesindia.com/article/covid19-frontline-warriors/
this-social-worker-from-lucknow-cremates-covid19-victims-for-
free/68047/1

United Saints Recovery Project. HandsOn New Orleans. Retrieved April
16, 2025, from
https://volunteer.handsonneworleans.org/agency/detail/?agen-
cy_id=99693

Uruguay ex-president Jose Mujica diagnosed with 'challenging' cancer.
(2024, April 29). Reuters. Retrieved from
https://www.reuters.com/world/americas/uruguay-ex-presi-
dent-jose-mujica-diagnosed-with-challenging-cancer-2024-04-29/

What is Spiritual Surrender? Know the Value of...
https://www.ananda.org/blog/spiritual-surrender/

What's Needed in Our Digital Lives: The Virtue of Humility.
https://www.psychologytoday.com/us/blog/virtue-in-the-me-
dia-world/202412/whats-needed-in-our-digital-lives-the-virtue-
of-humility

Why Is It Important to Stay Humble? – Verywell Mind.
https://www.verywellmind.com/why-is-it-important-to-be-hum-
ble-5223266

Wong, C. (2022, April 8). Despite being partially deaf, this musician travelled to 102 countries alone & set a M'sian record. Wau Post. Retrieved from https://waupost.com/despite-being-partially-deaf-this-musician-travelled-to-102-countries-alone-set-a-msian-record/

Worthington Jr., Everett L., et al. "Humility: The Quiet Virtue that Strengthens Psychological Flexibility." Journal of Contextual Behavioral Science, 6(1), 2017, pp. 41–51.

Zimmerman, Neia. "Fellow Runner Helps Competitor Finish High School Final Race in Act of Sportsmanship." ABC News, November 13, 2024. https://abcnews.go.com/GMA/Living/fellow-runner-helps-competitor-finish-high-school-final-race/story?id=115901418